Dr. Joan Faro

I'll remember your
professionalism and your
kindness.
Keep curing and caring.

Warren Reed
10/29/86

WARREN H. REED

POSITIVE LISTENING

LEARNING TO HEAR WHAT PEOPLE ARE REALLY SAYING

FRANKLIN WATTS

New York   Toronto

1985

Library of Congress Cataloging in Publication Data

Reed, Warren H.
Positive listening.

Includes index.
1. Communication in management. 2. Executive ability.
3. Listening. I. Title.
HD03.3.R44   1985   658.4'52   85-11470
ISBN 0-531-09583-5

ACKNOWLEDGMENTS

My sincerest thanks to Stuart Nordheimer, Manager, New York Marketing Services, Quotron Systems, Inc., for his assistance in developing case studies used in this book; to Steve Wells for his constructive, spontaneous editorial comments during the writing; to all the students in universities and business schools who helped me become a better listener through their expressions of confidence in themselves; and to Bill Newton, Senior Editor at Franklin Watts, and his staff for their editorial guidance.

FOREWORD

The premise of this book is that listening gets results. The purpose of the book is to get managers listening. We'd all agree that the premise is right, but very few of us really know how to get that job done. The book will help you practice what is perhaps the single greatest need in business, getting results through good communication.

The business I know best, the investment services industry, has at its heart meeting the needs and goals of investors. Not often is this business described as a listening business. We've found, however, that effectively meeting clients' needs for quality and service is achieved only to the degree that our investment executives respond to clients by listening.

While producing quality results in my particular business pivots on good listening techniques, I'll wager the same is true—and probably to the same degree—in your business. At every level in a company the success of executives depends on building the tools for effective action. That action begins with what Warren Reed calls "positive listening."

If managers already knew and used the techniques of positive listening, I'd wager that corporate culture would have a very different nature than the one we presently see. But the point we must recognize is that very few managers have mastered the answers to their biggest problem, in fact, very few recognize that the problem is indeed a listening problem.

The solutions are now available to you. Positive listening has the capacity to improve your performance and the performance of the people who work for you. Positive listening gets results. And this book gets that process started. All managers will welcome Warren Reed's techniques.

Don Nickelson
President
Paine Webber Consumer Markets

PREFACE

Several months ago I convinced myself that there was a need for a new approach to listening in business that would help managers be more successful in their jobs. I believed, like so many others, that listening was fundamentally an exercise in filtering out unwanted, nonrelevant information and ideas while simultaneously understanding or retaining that which was meaningful and useful. This put the emphasis on the manager as a processor of information, but not necessarily as a controller of the input.

Think about that for a moment! You, as a manager, are expected to be in control of any and all situations on the job. Yet when you listen to others you seem to have fewer opportunities to do this. I wanted to find a new way to help managers get results by being good listeners and good managers at the same time.

While researching "listening" at the library a short time ago, my exchange with the librarian put my thinking in perspective at last. Here's what happened:

Librarian:	Good morning! May I help you?
Me:	Yes, thank you! My name is Warren Reed. I'm a management consultant. I'm preparing a course on listening and would like to see your periodical file.
Librarian:	On what subject?
Me:	(Trying to hide my surprise and consternation at this kind of response) On listening.
Librarian:	Thank you!

Even after the librarian brought me a substantial quantity of folders and I began examining the contents, I still couldn't shake the incident. I reviewed what I'd said and pondered why the librarian hadn't heard correctly.

Then it hit me! I realized I was the guilty party in that curious exchange. The librarian was innocent. I wasn't the victim of the librarian's failure to listen; the librarian was the victim of my failure to communicate.

Suppose, I imagined, our exchange had gone something like this:

Librarian:	Good morning! May I help you?
Me:	Yes, thank you! May I see your periodical file on listening.
Librarian:	Certainly!

How simple! How obvious! Going back over our original dialogue, I realized my opening remarks were superfluous and irrelevant. The librarian had to wade through extraneous information to hear what I really wanted to say.

Embarrassing? Yes! In retrospect, though, I'm glad it happened. That incident helped me get to the heart of my new course and gave impetus to this book. It confirmed for me that listening involves more than merely "hearing" what is said.

Listening is a two-way communications process where you, the manager, have the obligation and the power to help yourself, your employees, your customers, and others communicate effectively. This process, called *positive listening*, puts the emphasis on how you use your listening skills to get results in your job.

Managers who are positive listeners achieve an infinite number of rewards that add to their income and personal success. All it takes is a desire to learn why listening is important to you and a belief that you are ready to enjoy the benefits of *positive listening*. Let's explore, together, how this will happen by getting control of listening on the job.

CONTENTS

POSITIVE LISTENING

WHY LISTENING IS IMPORTANT
TO YOU, THE MANAGER

Chapter 1 goals:

Prepare you to take a serious look at your listening effectiveness and its consequences on your performance.

Demonstrate that listening is critical to your success.

BEGIN WITH THINGS
THAT ARE SELF-EVIDENT

You listen to people every working day. You listen to the boss, your employees, peers, customers, vendors, and others. In addition, all of them listen to you.

In any given interchange between you and a business associate, circumstances may require that you do most of the listening. On other occasions the situation is reversed, and others spend the majority of their time listening to you. Quite often, listening may be shared about equally, with you as both sender and receiver.

In short, when you deal with people inside or outside the organization, neither you nor your associates can escape involvement in the listening process.

KEY FACTS ABOUT
LISTENING IN BUSINESS

Experts estimate that managers spend close to 50 percent of the working day listening. That's about equal to the

EXHIBIT 1A

How Managers Spend Their Communications Time

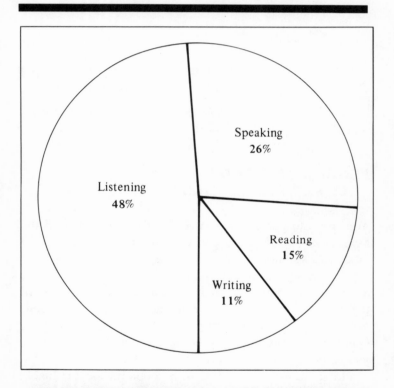

Source: Listening: A Guide to Effective Communications Management. A Warren H. Reed, Consultants course.

combined time managers spend speaking, writing, and reading as illustrated in the chart at left.

This time factor alone is sufficient cause for a serious examination of your listening efficiency. But there's more to it than that.

According to a recent survey of 250 Fortune 500 companies, the majority of managers are not considered effective listeners.[1] When employees were asked "What is your impression of the typical manager in the organization?" the results indicated that 64 percent of the managers were thought to lack training in good listening techniques. Is it possible that you are one of those managers? That's an exceedingly high percentage of managers who are thought to be deficient listeners!

What's also frightening is that listening experts also place the cost of poor listening practices in business at billions of dollars each year. That's a harrowing figure to contemplate.

As a result of these estimates, and the aforementioned Fortune 500 study, higher management has become increasingly aware of the need to turn things around. They believe more and more that listening skills are crucial to job performance and are demanding that managers do something about it. Listening can no longer be sloughed off as just one more item in the vocabulary of communications.

In today's business world the consequences of indifferent listening are awesome to contemplate:

unresolved problems

overlooked solutions

ineffectual decisions

costly errors

unattempted projects

ignored suggestions

unkept appointments

misinterpreted ideas and information

unsolicited points of view

poor morale

unplaced customer orders

Poor listening may result in serious problems for managers in handling customer and employee relations. For instance, customers may become disenchanted (for every customer who tells a manager that he or she is unhappy, there are three or four others who keep such information to themselves and end up taking their business elsewhere); employees may perform below standard or give minimum effort, thereby affecting production in a negative way.

These are some of the countless ways that ineffective listening may inhibit the performance of any manager. On the other hand, the consequences of effective listening are powerful indeed:

willingness to express ideas

interest in sharing information

greater conviction and believability

increased understanding and trust

stronger desire to achieve and excel

recognition of superior effort

These are significant motivators that help managers and employees obtain satisfaction and rewards from their jobs.

There may be other factors besides listening that lead to these desirable consequences; however, listening is believed to be a primary ingredient in their attainment.

WHAT YOU CAN DO TO ASSURE YOUR LISTENING COMPETENCY

In later chapters you'll examine the steps to follow to build your listening skills, and you'll see how to use *positive listening* in your job. First, you should take a close look at your current job and determine where listening plays a key role. Here's how to do this:

On a sheet of paper, record your job responsibilities as you see them. Then rate listening as a factor in relation to each of these items. It doesn't matter whether you're the sender or the receiver of the communication, or listening most of the time or part of the time. Merely consider if listening takes place, and how important it is to you in performing your job.

Keep in mind that the purpose of this exercise is to help you see how listening fits into your job. Besides, you'll need this checklist to get ready to do something about putting your listening skills into regular practice. In Chapter Ten you'll return to this list when you prepare an action plan for using *positive listening* in your job.

The headings for your checklist might look something like the one shown in Exhibit 1B. In fact, to help you get started, a typical element of most managers jobs is given as an illustration.

The ratings you assign to each item may depend on any number of related elements. Chief among these would be the frequency of the communication. For instance, suppose most of your subordinates work in the field. This may re-

Exhibit 1B

Manager's Job Responsibilities	Listening is:		
	Critically Relevant	**Usually Relevant**	**Seldom Relevant**
	(PLACE AN "X" IN THE APPROPRIATE COLUMN ALONGSIDE EACH ITEM)		

Telephone Communications

   . . . with the boss

   . . . with subordinates

   . . . with peers

   . . . with customers

   . . . with vendors

quire that you and your staff do most of your business by phone, thereby resulting in a "critically relevant" rating.

Also, although contacts might not be frequent, the nature of the communication might influence the rating. Example:

The boss doesn't phone many times but when he does it normally concerns top priority matters that require discussion and settlement promptly. Listening skills, therefore, are significant, even though the activity is infrequent.

After preparing your list and rating the listening factor for each element of your job, compare it with Exhibit 1C. This comparison will help you be certain that you did not exclude any of your job responsibilities. In fairness to yourself, however, make your list first, before you move on.

Your Job Inventory—
What Does It Tell You
About Listening?

As indicated earlier, managers are thought to spend about 50 percent of their time listening. Now that you've prepared your list of job responsibilities, you can make your own time estimate. How much time do you spend listening?

Chances are you discovered from your analysis that your listening time may be higher than 50 percent. There's a good reason for that.

As you rise in management, listening tends to become a higher priority. When your job grows in complexity and diversity, you become more reliant on other people for information and ideas that help you make decisions and take action. Also, you find that your chief role is that of an administrator, an overseer of events and activities, instead of the traditional "doer."

To illustrate and highlight this dependency on listening, consider the behavior of a manager of a department who is responsible for installing a new automated system in his company.

With the help of his staff he develops an action plan for implementing the new system, establishing timetables, schedules, methods for measuring results, etc., that will meet established objectives. Since he needs to know what's happening at each stage of the installation process, feedback becomes the key ingredient for determining what is going on at all times.

The feedback comes to him in different forms: written reports, analyses and interpretations of computerized records, and, of course, meetings with his staff and other key people to review progress and outcomes.

The meetings may be formal or informal, lengthy, brief, frequent or infrequent. Regardless of the form or duration of these meetings, the manager knows that the input he receives helps him determine if results have been achieved and, if not, what to do next. He listens to identify and resolve problems, understand and interpret how people are adapting to the new system, learning how his staff is dealing with the task at hand and how they may be coping with situations that test their mettle, and more.

CLARIFYING YOUR PERSPECTIVE ON LISTENING

So far you've taken a clinical look at the reasons why it is important for you to listen. The job inventory exercise should have helped convince you that perfecting your listening skills should be one of your top priorities. In fact, you may already be convinced that you've got sound reasons for getting started on learning and practicing the skills of *positive listening*.

At the same time you may also be thinking that listening is not the easiest of tasks to carry off successfully. You're not only justified in feeling this way, you've got support from other quarters.

Scientists have found that you must break concentration or focus every two to five seconds. It is not unusual or peculiar to find yourself, or someone else, dwelling on other things while listening.

Also, retention is a problem. How much of a spoken message can one retain over a period of time without losing touch with the essential ideas? Some experts maintain we retain a mere 20 percent of what we hear. These, as well as other factors, make listening a real challenge especially to you, the manager, who needs control over the listening process to do an effective job.

Exhibit 1C

Job Inventory Checklist

Manager's Job Responsibilities	Listening is:		
	Critically Relevant	Usually Relevant	Seldom Relevant
	(PLACE AN "X" IN THE APPROPRIATE COLUMN ALONGSIDE EACH ITEM)		

Telephone Communications

   ... with the boss

   ... with subordinates

   ... with peers

   ... with customers

   ... with vendors

Holding Informal Discussions with Employees Re Work/Work Problems

Delegating Work

Appraising Employee Performance ... conducting interviews

Person-to-Person Contacts with Customers

Person-to-Person Contacts with Vendors

Interviewing Job Applicants

Coaching Employees

Counseling Employees

Attending Meetings/ Conferences/Seminars

What is Positive Listening?

Positive listening refers to the way you look at listening as a means of being effective in your job. It is a critical aspect of your interpersonal skills that involves the way you look at your own needs, as well as the approaches you use to communicate with people. There is no ready-made formula to follow. It's all wrapped up in having a personal commitment to succeed at the things you do and understanding that to listen well helps you and others communicate effectively.

Positive listening is probably the single most reliable interpersonal skill a manager can master. Your next step in appreciating its applications is to take a long, hard look at your current listening habits and plan to overcome the barriers that often impede your ability to be effective. Once that is accomplished you'll be ready to let *positive listening* begin to work for you.

NOTES

1. Glen M. Morgan, "Therapeutic Listening—A Communication Tool," *Training and Development Journal*, copyright 1983, American Society for Training and Development.

2

GETTING CONTROL
OF LISTENING:
WHERE DO YOU BEGIN?

Chapter 2 goals:

Help you take a look at your current attitude toward listening and determine where you excel and what deficiencies require your attention.

Identify the barriers that often impede listening effectiveness, then determine how you can overcome these barriers and get control of listening.

If one of your employees were to tell you that you were not a very good listener, chances are you would be taken aback by the bluntness, as well as the presumptuousness, of such a statement. Provocative comments of this sort tend to produce defensive reactions. Most managers like to believe that they listen well, and they want others to feel the same way.

More than likely your staff will not volunteer such information even if they believe your listening skills are wanting. Telling the boss he or she is deficient at something is not quite the politic thing to do. So don't expect to be told such things. In some ways that's a disadvantage to you because you can't deal with a problem if you don't think it exists.

Nevertheless, now that you are more keenly aware of where you spend your listening time on the job, perhaps you feel the need to look more closely at how well you listen. Just think, if all those managers cited earlier as ineffective listeners improved their listening skills by only a fraction what a positive impact that would have on their performance.

Most managers would probably prefer to think of themselves as good listeners. It's safer to take a clear look at one's current attitudes toward listening and come to grips with what needs changing. It stands to reason that if so much of a manager's time is spent listening, there's no room for complacency or overconfidence.

EVALUATING YOUR ATTITUDE TOWARD LISTENING

You can evaluate some aspects of your current attitude toward listening by examining ten key questions. As you respond "yes" or "no" to these questions that were compiled from selected listening questionnaires, try to be completely objective. You and you alone, in this instance, are passing judgment on your listening ability. Unless your response is an unqualified "yes," then make "no" your answer. Please answer these questions now.

How did you do? Were you completely honest with yourself? Were certain questions tougher to deal with than others? Now, look again at these questions, only this time from a slightly different perspective. This time, as you reread each one, ask yourself what you believe are the positive consequences of each affirmative response.

EXAMINING YOUR PRESENT STRENGTHS AND DEFICIENCIES

How Do I Measure Up as a Listener?

		Yes	No
1.	Do I try to encourage others to participate in the discussion?	___	___
2.	Do I look at the other person when he or she talks with me?	___	___
3.	Do I listen to understand rather than spend the time preparing my next remark?	___	___
4.	Do I allow others to express their complete thoughts without interrupting?	___	___
5.	Do I guard against assuming I know what others mean or how they feel by asking them questions to assure understanding?	___	___
6.	Do I avoid becoming hostile or excited when another's views differ from my own?	___	___
7.	Do I try to summarize points of agreement or disagreement?	___	___
8.	In recording a message do I concentrate on writing key ideas rather than getting down all the facts?	___	___
9.	Do I ignore distractions when listening?	___	___
10.	Do I refrain from tuning out someone because the message is dull or boring, or because I do not personally know or like him or her?	___	___

EXAMINING YOUR PRESENT STRENGTHS AND DEFICIENCIES

More than likely you responded with an unqualified "yes" to a number of the questions. Start with these, since you already have them under control. For each "yes" response, think of the results you achieve when you take the action— these are the positive consequences. Do the same with the "no's" as if you had answered "yes."

To help you benefit from this exercise enter your positive consequences in the column with that heading for each item. An example is given as a guide for item number one. Substitute your own, if yours is more appropriate. Then, compare your positive consequences with those that follow. You may find your commentary on some of the factors similar to those on the listing and, of course, you'll find that you have added new ones as well.

LISTENING DISCIPLINE	*POSITIVE CONSEQUENCES*
When I speak with others, I encourage them to participate in the discussion.	The more input and feedback I get, the greater the chances for mutual understanding.
I look at the other person when he or she speaks with me.	
I listen to understand rather than preparing my next remark.	

LISTENING DISCIPLINE   *POSITIVE CONSEQUENCES*

I allow others to express
their complete thoughts
without interrupting.

I guard against assuming
I know what others
mean or how they feel
by asking them
questions to assure
understanding.

I avoid becoming hostile
or excited when
another's view differs
from my own.

I try to summarize
points of agreement and
disagreement.

When I record a
message I concentrate on
writing key ideas rather
than getting down all the
facts.

I ignore distractions
when listening.

I refrain from tuning out
someone because the
message is dull or
boring, or because I do
not personally know or
like him or her.

LISTENING DISCIPLINE	*POSITIVE CONSEQUENCES*
When I speak with others, I encourage them to participate in the discussion.	The more input and feedback I get, the greater the chances for mutual understanding.
I look at the other person when he or she speaks with me.	My eye contact conveys my interest in the person. It also helps me focus on how he or she reacts to what we are discussing.
I listen to understand rather than preparing my next remark.	I concentrate on what the other person is saying/doing and thereby better appreciate his/her point of view.
I allow others to express their complete thoughts without interrupting.	I seldom miss important ideas or information, and I don't run the risk of stifling communication.
I guard against assuming I know what others mean or how they feel by asking them questions to assure understanding.	I can help direct the discussion so that we focus on meaningful elements.
I try to summarize points of agreement or disagreement.	My summaries promote understanding and help me be certain I have not overlooked valuable information the other person has given.

LISTENING DISCIPLINE	*POSITIVE CONSEQUENCES*
I avoid becoming hostile or excited when another's view differs from my own.	By constraining the emotional aspects, I can deal with situations on a more factual basis and stay on target.
When I record a message I concentrate on writing key ideas rather than getting down all the facts.	This helps me avoid getting bogged down in detail; my emphasis is always on central ideas related to the topic.
I ignore distractions when listening.	The person I'm speaking with realizes that he/she and our topic are my primary concerns.
I refrain from tuning out someone because the message is dull or boring, or because I do not personally know or like him or her.	I am better at weeding out the important from the unimportant by concentrating on the complete message.

This exercise was designed primarily to raise your consciousness level about listening practices that help you in your job. The greater your awareness of the payoff in improving communications, the more purposeful you'll be in making them work.

Here are some things to do to get your listening practices under control:

- Be totally honest with yourself about what you do well and what you don't do well. Your objectivity is the key to your willingness to change the kinds of behavior that may inhibit your performance.

- Capitalize on your strengths (your current listening efficiencies) and watch out for those things with which you have trouble. Deal with deficiencies as if they had to be corrected to prevent serious problems. For example, suppose you seldom make summary statements to ensure understanding. Start practicing these in your discussions with others. Take time to note the results. When you consciously strive to interject summary statements into the conversation at appropriate times, you'll find yourself listening for key ideas so that your summaries are always accurate and useful. Begin trying this in your next discussion.

(A more complete analysis of the summary statement technique will be addressed in Chapter Five.)

It usually isn't too difficult to identify a communications need and find a solution that seems correct, just as you did in the above exercise. On paper it looks as if you can move right along and get the job done just as you planned.

Keep in mind, however, that listening is a tough business requiring perception and daily practice of the required skills. It is impractical to be casual and neglect fundamental responsibilities, so don't lull yourself into a state of false security. It's what you do every day on the job that counts.

IDENTIFYING THE BARRIERS
TO EFFECTIVE LISTENING

Now that you have a good idea about your attitude toward listening and have identified your strengths and weaknesses, you should be ready to take charge of your listening development through an examination of the barriers to effective listening.

Managers face numerous barriers to listening. All of these can be challenged and, through conscious, persistent effort, eventually overcome. Some are naturally a lot tougher than others to root out. To lick any barrier, a special kind of perseverence is needed that succeeds when it is consistently followed over a period of time.

Right now, at the start of your analysis, it's wise to identify every barrier you believe you face. The reason for doing this is simple: *Any and all barriers prevent you from listening objectively and intelligently to others.*

When listening is impeded, you lose concentration. You end up dwelling on things that inhibit your ability to communicate. Unless listening barriers are eliminated or controlled, you may miss important information, misinterpret fact and opinion, and, most important, lose out on opportunities to act where you and the other person may benefit. In short, you can't do your job as well as it should be done while barriers persist and prevent you from being a positive listener.

Let's examine a typical barrier that you and every other manager has had to wrestle with in one way or another at some time—the use, by the speaker, of a word or phrase that triggers negative reactions. When this occurs during the course of a conversation or presentation you immediately feel uncomfortable. You may be inhibited to such an extent that anything else said by that person, no matter how relevant to the discussion and no matter how logical, is missed or misinterpreted. You find yourself in a state of mind where you are too preoccupied with your own thoughts to pay much attention to what is said subsequently. You may even react so negatively that you overtly reveal your distress by objecting strenuously on the spot. Suddenly you and the speaker, and others if they are present, move far away from the main topic and are thrust into a new and perhaps irrelevant discussion or argument centered on emotional feelings. In such situations, things seem to get worse rather than better.

If you don't voice your disapproval outright, you may find that you hear or understand very little else that is said, or perhaps contribute less because you spend your time reflecting on your distress, or wrestle (often subconsciously) with your own problem in dealing with the unpleasant feelings generated which you wish could be controlled.

This is one of the listening barriers that some managers may find difficult to handle. It takes a superior effort to control your reaction to trigger words if they tend to dominate or unduly influence your behavior.

Also, consider that it may be you who uses a trigger word or phrase that gets these kinds of reactions from the person with whom you are speaking. In such cases you must look for and be able to recognize clues that signify discontent—a sudden dropping out of the conversation, the other person's looking away, a change of expression (a frown, for instance), the shifting of one's physical position, finger tapping, or outright silence. There are all sorts of ways in which one conveys annoyance or apprehension.

Worse yet are situations in which managers let these clues go unnoticed or otherwise demonstrate limited concern for the other person's feelings and reactions. Blithely they move on, ignoring or overlooking what is happening and, in the process, stifling listening attempts.

Our main point here, however, is that as a listener you've got to control your response in such a way that you don't alienate the speaker, who may then withhold information that is of value to you. You must learn to deal with such elements of a conversation in a way that the discussion continues until its logical conclusion, with both parties achieving the ultimate benefit from what is said.

You've got to take charge of things that get in the way of listening. You do this first by understanding why barriers must be broken down and dealt with. You can't listen for meaning and identify central ideas when a number of things prevent you from accomplishing this even before the speaker utters one word.

Your Personal Checklist of Listening Barriers

At this point think of things that get in your way of listening to someone. As an example, "distractions" would be considered a common listening barrier. When broken down into specific types of distractions, you end up with a formidable list that can be used to help you assess how well you deal with them.

Telephone interruptions are a common distraction. It may be the sound of the phone that is distracting, although most managers probably will say that they've gotten used to it and can safely ignore the sound itself when they have to. Usually it's the result of the call being received either by you, the person with whom you are conversing (if either of you take the time to answer the phone), or a secretary or someone else in the office or plant who answers, then interrupts with a message.

Barriers tend to fall into various categories. They may be semantic, emotional, physical, personal, psychological, or a combination of these elements. These barriers tend to remain with us when we blame them on events and other people rather than ourselves.

You will be able to eliminate or control any barrier when

you believe that *you* create most of them and can do something to overcome them.

You shouldn't have any trouble identifying those barriers that get in your way. Refer to the ten key questions you answered earlier to uncover several of them. Also, some may be found among those on this list of common barriers faced by managers:

• Distractions	May occur as interruptions during a conversation or meeting; poor acoustics; noises; cross-conversations; others speaking within hearing distance; persons moving about a room; telephones ringing and being answered, etc.
• Trigger Words	Words, phrases, ideas that provoke a negative response and lead you away from the main topic.
• Vocabulary	Unfamiliarity with the speaker's use of the language. May be specific words, phrasing, accent, etc.
• Listless or Indifferent Responses	Failure to give overt reactions to what is being said, thereby inhibiting or stifling feedback. Occurs

	as blank expression, lack of questions to clarify issues/ideas/information and keep discussion moving and on target.
• Writing Down Everything	Excessive note-taking, with resultant inability to keep up with what is being said or give speaker proper attention.
• Limited Attention Span	Lack of desire to accept or comprehend new or unusual ideas/information; dislike of speaker; disinterest in topic; daydreaming, etc.

TAKING STEPS TO OVERCOME LISTENING BARRIERS

You just can't wave a wand and eliminate impediments to listening. Why not choose a few barriers that can be challenged and changed? It is hoped that you'll select the ones that are most persistent and not necessarily the easiest ones to control.

Select these barriers from the preceding list, as well as others that come to mind. Spell out, preferably in writing, what you'll do to control the barrier. Remember, you'll succeed best by attacking those that *you* create.

For starters, here's an example of what you might do should you choose telephone interruptions as a key distraction.

Listening Barrier	*Ways to Overcome Barrier*
The telephone	Don't answer; arrange beforehand for someone to screen calls and interrupt only if message is urgent or don't interrupt at all. Hold discussion with employee or customer in area where there are no phones. Select a time and place to hold discussion when you are least likely to be interrupted by the phone (in certain businesses incoming calls tend to cluster at certain times of the day).
	If you are in someone else's office and he/she is interrupted by calls, take this time to review your notes or thoughts and compose comments or questions relative to the discussion.

Go after your barriers vigorously and you'll form habits that help make you a superior listener and a better manager.

POSITIVE LISTENING
AS A MANAGEMENT FORCE

Chapter 3 goals:

Demonstrate that when you make listening a priority skill it improves your performance and the performance of others.

Help you understand the value of controlling listening with all levels of the organization. You'll see how you can integrate your management style with the organization's style to get the best results.

MAKING LISTENING AN
ORGANIZATIONAL PRIORITY

Successful managers—those who consistently get good results in their jobs—have a commitment to excellence. It's a common commitment successful managers share regardless of what type of job they hold, the size of the organization, or who they supervise. This commitment is nurtured by their need for achievement and recognition, their understanding of the management process (planning, organizing, directing, controlling, and evaluating), and their perceptive appreciation of the human element in business (being fair, expressing empathy, permitting freedom within the structure where appropriate), etc.

Can managers who have this commitment be passive listeners? What do you think?

Chances are you believe there is a strong correlation between good management and effective listening. You'll make listening an automatic priority when you have a purpose in your job, set attainable objectives, keep your boss and your staff informed about what's needed and what's going on, show high expectations of yourself and others. Your disposition toward your job sets the tone for any and all communications. Listening then becomes an integral part of the total job because your personal standards of performance require this.

How Managers Benefit From Listening

When you're considered a good listener others more readily share information and ideas with you. In turn they want to listen to you because they respect your ability as a manager and value your interest in them. This healthy cross-communication climate brings you benefits that help you do your job.

A good listening outlook:

- Fosters mutual respect.

- Promotes cooperation and support.

- Reduces tension and stress.

- Stimulates group solidarity.

- Encourages the surfacing of real issues, as opposed to those that are prefabricated or misleading.

In addition, when a manager makes listening a priority:

- Projects are likely to be undertaken willingly because employees understand how and why they are contributing.

- Employees tend to set their own standards for performance, which are sometimes higher than published standards.

- People generally come to you of their own free will when there's a problem that they cannot resolve on their own.

- Conflict is more likely to result from work issues, not fear and anxiety. Since work issues are dealt with in a constructive manner, there is a greater opportunity to resolve them satisfactorily.

- You find that others tell you things that are more relevant and meaningful to the subject at hand. As a result you substantially reduce the need to expend energy reading between the lines of what is said to uncover hidden meanings.

When you're motivated to listen better you increase your chances of becoming a more effective manager. When you work at becoming an effective manager you listen better. Whichever way you go, you stand to gain.

To illustrate the management approach that relies on listening as a positive force, take the case of a manager who is transferred or promoted from one department to another. Ineffective managers will introduce themselves to their new group by keeping a low profile and issuing statements about the work in memo form. Personal contact is limited deliberately. The game plan seems to be "Keep them guessing and people will work hard to protect themselves."

On the other hand, effective managers might take the following steps to get acquainted with the work and the people:

- Hold a staff meeting to introduce themselves and greet the employees with whom they'll be working.

- Set the tone for their working relationship by: (1) briefly stating their position about their reliance on them; (2) conveying a positive attitude about the group's contributions to the department; (3) discussing what they hope to accomplish with employee support.

- Schedule individual meetings right away with each person to learn more about what they do and what they believe are the most important things about their jobs. (The intent of these meetings would have been revealed at the staff session.) Listen attentively at the meetings, taking notes and getting back to each person on individual items of concern.

It is easy to see that the listening process is a critical element of these initial communications where the establishment of rapport and authority sets the stage for the relationship. By making listening a priority, employees are encouraged to speak freely as well as listen to what the manager has to say.

CONTROLLING YOUR COMMUNICATIONS WITH OTHERS

Your commitment to achieve results helps you appreciate the need to exercise control over your communications. Control is a key ingredient in listening. It simply means that you consciously guide and direct your discussions with others so that you have a meaningful exchange of ideas and information. You listen actively, aware of why you are listening as well as how you are listening for significant thought.

Control simply implies that you are on top of things. It rules out indifference, the most gnawingly negative ingredient that could inhibit the effectiveness of any communication.

This deliberate control takes many forms. For example, in speaking with a subordinate on any subject, you guide the conversation in a number of ways. Your questions help keep the discussion on target (related to the subject) and encourage the employee to contribute to the discussion. Your interest in the person and what he or she has to say is also conveyed through eye contact. By being visually alert you show that you are attentive, as well as sensitive to the other person's point of view. In addition, eye contact enables you to detect physical (nonverbal) clues that indicate possible changes in behavior. Succeeding chapters will cover these subjects in depth.

You can also control your communications by exercising limited control. Suppose, for instance, that you decide that a particular project requires that your subordinates have complete freedom of choice in selecting the method, materials, or means of completing the project successfully. Your decision to go this route may be based on one or more of the following factors:

• The way you assess the situation itself. In this case the nature of the project—its complexity, relevance to the work effort, timeliness, et al.

• The needs of the group. You may believe that certain persons may make particularly worthwhile contributions where they're given free reign.

- Your own needs or requirements. You may decide that time constraints limit or prohibit your own participation, or you may decide to find out how your employees can deal with a complex problem on their own. In the latter case your motivation may be linked to your desire to aid in their personal development by giving them a chance to show what they can do on their own initiative with only limited guidance.

When you practice downward listening your sensitivity to your position of authority can be a significant factor in how well both you and your subordinate listen. The sensitive manager uses authority in a positive way. Although there is seldom any doubt about who is in charge, the manager makes certain the employee does not feel intimidated. Instead, the manager conveys a supportive attitude that clearly shows respect for the individual and his/her work. It's as if you and the employee have formed a kind of partnership through your mutual commitment to achieve results.

This partnership concept carries over to your communications with the boss and senior management. It is clearly your responsibility to understand general practices and codes of behavior required by the organization. You also need to be familiar with the organization's goals and appreciate how they affect you.

In direct contacts with your boss your listening practices are not much different from what you'd follow with subordinates. Eye contact, for instance, is equally significant. About the only major difference is in your skill in directing questions to the boss in a tactful and diplomatic way.

When the need to get the job done well is of paramount importance to you, you won't hesitate to ask clarifying questions of the boss. If you have established a "partnership" relationship your superior will see your perseverance and interest as a sign that you really do have a commitment to excellence.

Your motivation is what prompts the action you take in any situation. Your inclination to control or guide your communications with others is enhanced when there's a definite purpose in mind, a goal in sight, a substantial need to be met.

To demonstrate this sense of urgency, or need, that influences how well one listens, take the case of the manager responding to a telephone call from someone whose intent is to sell a product or service. If the manager views the call as an unwanted, unnecessary, time-impinging interruption of his routine, he may listen to what is said halfheartedly or indifferently. Sales callers who practice telemarketing techniques are careful to find ways to arouse interest immediately, so we will listen.

Also, when you're at a cocktail party and are introduced to a number of guests, how quickly you may tend to forget, or ignore, their names and almost anything about them. The atmosphere, with its constant buzzing, fast-paced chatter, and drinking tends to detract from one's interest in listening attentively. As a result you may not try too hard to listen well.

But what if you're at a cocktail party and you've got a genuine purpose for being there beyond mere socializing. Imagine yourself a sales manager and many of the persons invited to the party as potential buyers or distributors of your product or service. Or suppose you are running for political office in your community and the persons attending the party are in a position to support you. Do you listen for names and information with greater care under these circumstances? Watch how successfully you rise to the challenge when the chips are on the line.

Your behavior toward all levels inside the organization

(boss, subordinates, peers) and business persons outside the organization (prospects, customers, vendors, professional colleagues) generally is a combined product of:

* Your basic management temperament (the behavioral style that suits your personality).

* What your organization expects of you (the prescribed policies and the culture).

* How you view each situation as it occurs.

THE EFFECT OF YOUR MANAGEMENT STYLE ON LISTENING

Just as your commitment to excellence influences your desire to listen effectively, so does your basic management or leadership style. For that reason it's important for you to examine your style and determine whether or not it has a positive influence on your ability to listen.

Most experts agree that the most favorable style is one that has a healthy mix of task orientation and people orientation. You might agree with this if you believe that a manager is judged on his or her ability to get people to meet objectives that lead to greater production (higher profitability).

On the whole, however, managers tend to lean toward following one particular style of managing.[1] For instance, some managers are more comfortable in one-on-one encounters. They appear to be more persuasive when they and an employee, boss, peer, or someone outside the organization reach agreement on issues by talking things over, usually face-to-face. The warm, friendly atmosphere is their cup of tea. Individual, as well as group participation in decision-making is important to them, not necessarily because they believe someone else has a better way than their own, but because winning people over to their side is a key factor in their dealings with others. A strong desire to be liked may be a motivating factor in their adherence to this approach.

Other managers have a strong need to make decisions for the group. They tend to believe that participatory exercises, where employees or bosses share in the decision-making process is too time consuming, take away from their authority and don't get good results. Their single most obsessive fear is that others will see their relinquishing control at any time as a sign of weakness.

Still a third group of managers tend to withhold making decisions until they get input from almost any other source. They fear failure so much that they are unwilling to risk making the decision by themselves. If something goes wrong they may be self-critical for being dependent on others or may blame others for having provided unworkable advice. These are the types who, when eating in a restaurant, may wait for others in their party to order, then choose an item for themselves that someone else has already selected. They do not wish to go it alone.

A fourth group tends to be self-reliant and independent, preferring to go their own way. The primary difference between these managers and those who wish to make decisions for others is that the independent type is more iconoclastic. He'll stick his neck out and buck the system to show he's right, whereas managers who prefer to be in command generally are enforcers of the system. For example, if there's a dress code established for the company, the command type of manager will not only conform himself but insist that others do the same; the self-reliant type often will be indifferent to the code and may even dress in opposition to what is preferred by the company.

All of these types may have moderate to great success doing things their way. Much depends, of course, on how others respond to their styles. When these styles are accepted, or if they work, there's less tendency to see any need to change.

Yet in the long run managers who have good track records generally are those who can adapt their preferred styles to changing situations and the current needs of their people and the organization. An aggressive, outspoken, spontaneous type of manager would be foolish not to make a conscious effort to adjust his behavior when dealing with a boss who is deliberate, fastidious, and cautious.

According to Tannenbaum and Schmidt,[2] a successful leader is "one who maintains a high batting average in accurately assessing the forces that determine what his most appropriate behavior at any given time should be and in actually being able to behave accordingly."

The latter assessment of a manager's preferred behavior is a constructive one from a listening standpoint especially. It reinforces a practical belief that managers who are adaptable and flexible are also perceptive about what to do when communicating.

Effective listening demands that managers who adhere to any of the aforementioned behavioral styles be aware of how their styles affect their ability to listen. A reexamination of the description of all four of the styles probably makes it clear that each one could cause a problem in listening.

The best way to overcome any barriers that one's style might present is to make listening a priority. This conscious effort, which is part of your commitment to achieve results, makes the real difference. The key factor is your determination to control the listening process.

CONTROLLING TIME AND PLACE

Managers also exercise listening control when you consider that time and place are important aspects of the communications process. Look again at the job inventory you prepared in Chapter One. For each item that you listed determine the preferred time and place for that type of communication. If you do this you'll find that your sensitivity to the listening factor conditions you to try to control the environmental setting.

Ask yourself these questions to verify this sensitivity:

- Would you hold an appraisal interview at 4 P.M. on a Friday afternoon?

- Would you attempt to schedule a meeting with your boss shortly before he or she was to hold a critical conference with key persons in the organization (unless your input was needed for the conference)?

- Would you hold an interview with a job applicant in a nonprivate or semiprivate location where there might be interruptions or distractions?

- Would you conduct a large meeting attended by numerous prospects and customers in a place that is convenient for you but may be difficult for most attendees to reach?

You must ask yourself "When is the best time and where is the best place to talk so that you are assured that listening will take place on your part, and that the hour and the surroundings do not inhibit the other persons need or desire to listen."

Sometimes there are choices regarding time and place. Coaching sessions, for example, may be more beneficial from a listening standpoint if they are held at the employee's desk where the work is being performed, yet sometimes it is best to hold such a session in your office, where you require privacy.

How Physical Setting Affects Listening

A traditional seating arrangement in a business office often will find the manager seated at a desk with a chair adjacent to either the right or left and/or one or two chairs at the foot of the desk facing the manager. If space is not at a premium one is likely to find a separate area in the room where a table is surrounded by a few chairs. Nearby there may also be one or more separate conference rooms of different sizes and shapes for accommodating several persons.

The practical use of the physical setting can enhance the listening process. Today's manager, for instance, may be inclined to dispense with the chair by the side of the desk because the visitor may feel, psychologically, that under such circumstances he or she is not meeting the manager on equal terms. Often, managers who wish to avoid this type of uncomfortable feeling will move around in front of the desk and sit side by side or move to another area where the feeling of "equality" is enhanced.

Many other factors having to do with the physical setting also play a part in giving listening a green light. Among these factors are lighting, ventilation, degree of privacy (other persons not in the immediate area), smoking permitted or smoking not permitted, acoustics, noise, etc.

Where the physical setting is accommodating one is more likely to be able to concentrate on the content of the communication taking place. It stands to reason, then, that when managers take pains to make visitors comfortable, the climate they've provided is more conducive to listening.

Manager's Accessibility

"My door is always open!" How many times have managers made that statement? Numerous times, of course. It is the managers way of assuring others that he or she has an open ear and an open mind. Availability and accessibility are key ingredients in communicating. Employees, and others, may accept such a statement at face value or perhaps with a grain of salt. The extremes of reactions to a manager's announced open-door policy may range from "Whenever I have a problem my manager will take the time to hear me out—I like that" to "Sure, he says he's available at all times, but just try to get in to see him. He'll ask you to wait or tell you to come back another time."

The manager always sets the tone for what happens. When he makes himself accessible to others, and behaves this way consistently, his actions communicate to others that he is willing to listen to them. Then when he listens others are apt to treat him the same way—they're likely to listen to him. The realities of managerial life, however, often force the manager to "close the door" from time to time. Certain parts of the working day need to be set aside for planning or handling other duties in which privacy is critical to the accomplishment of the immediate task. In such cases the manager may not accept visitors or phone calls. To do their jobs effectively managers must create an acceptable mix of the open and the closed door—one where the balance demonstrates that the manager is being fair to everyone and gets the job done.

Regardless of the time and place, if listening is on your

priority list, you'll have little trouble determining how to handle this aspect of control.

With your commitment to results firmly fixed, an appreciation of the influence your management style has on listening, and an understanding that you can and must control your communications with others, you are prepared to move on to a discussion of the "how to" factors that are at the heart of *positive listening*.

NOTES

[1]For a complete discussion of the four management styles see Arthur Mortell, *The Anatomy of a Successful Salesman*, Copyright Farnsworth Publishing Company, Inc., Rockville Centre, N.Y.

[2]Reprinted by permission of the Harvard Business Review. Excerpt from "How to choose a leadership pattern" by Robert Tannenbaum and Warren H. Schmidt (May-June 1973). Copyright © 1973 by the President and Fellows of Harvard College; all rights reserved.

KNOWING WHAT TO
LISTEN FOR

Chapter 4 goals:

Describe how setting listening objectives helps you de-tect central ideas and keep the focus on the main intent of a communication; explore how note-taking in a desirable format aids retention; understand how you get more out of listening by defusing emotions, resisting biases, and avoiding distractions.

The well-organized manager identifies work priorities and concentrates on doing or delegating key tasks. This, of course, requires maximizing efforts to spend time productively: Activities for each day are planned carefully; un-planned-for events and activities are dealt with in light of the overall game plan for performing the job. These managers know that an unplanned day may end up being a chaotic day with energies spent on needless or unimportant tasks that perhaps should not have been attempted at all.

SETTING LISTENING OBJECTIVES

The manager who is a systematic work planner understands why it is important to plan to listen. Setting listening objectives is the first and foremost step in knowing what to listen for. If, generally, people retain only 20 percent of what is heard in a given exchange, managers can turn that around and increase the rate substantially by developing listening strategies.

What these strategies provide you is an opportunity to listen for meaning. When you're prepared to listen you'll detect central ideas more readily, because they are usually the main ideas for which you are looking. Also, if you're keyed to listening for what the speaker has to say and what you expect to hear, you are less likely to be disturbed by any form of distraction.

Going back to where the listening process takes root, getting ready to listen depends on your commitment to results. When you know what you want to achieve in any communication you'll know what kind of feedback you need.

A few examples of how managers prepare themselves to get the most out of listening ought to establish credibility for effective management of communications through planning.

Imagine that a manager decided that a staff member needed to learn more about data-processing systems and their function in order for the person to perform the job and interface more effectively with other persons in the organization.

The manager's first obligation would have been to speak with the employee about what was needed in the job, get the employee's input, then express his ideas about why he or she believed data-processing systems knowledge was important to the employee and the department.

Perhaps as a result of this dialogue, the manager gets agreement that the employee would benefit from taking a course at a local school or within the company (if one was offered). The step-by-step process followed might be something like this:

- Research the available courses and find one that closely approximates in purpose and content what is sought. The employee could do this, it could be worked on jointly, or the manager could delegate the assignment to another person or do it himself.

- Once a specific course is selected the manager would review the outline of the program with the employee, noting those aspects that he and the employee believe are most relevant/critical from a learning standpoint.

- The manager would finalize his thinking, then indicate in writing to the employee points of agreement about how the course will benefit him or her and the operation.

Upon completion of the course it would be important to hold a meeting with the employee to get feedback on what had been accomplished. The manager would probe for information about the benefits the employee had gotten from the course, where the employee believed knowledge applications could be made to the job, what steps he or she and the manager agreed should be taken to put the knowledge to work on the job.

Over a period of time the manager would follow through to determine the results, not so much to learn if the course itself was effective, but whether the work had improved and the employee was satisfied with the results.

However, suppose the manager had been indefinite about what was wanted and merely told the employee:

> "I've scheduled you to take a three-day course in data processing, here's the brochure [outline] showing what the course covers. This course will help you in your job."

Had this kind of sketchy approach been used, it is likely that the employee would have been uncertain about her purpose in attending the course and unsure of how the course might have benefitted her in her work. As a result, the employee may not have listened for those items most relevant to her job needs.

Another example: A manager has scheduled an appraisal interview with an employee. Regardless of what the estimate of the quality of the employee's current performance may be, how does the manager prepare for this meeting? Really effective managers take the time before the interview to review very carefully facts about the employee's performance and plan the interview accordingly. The manager's plan might look something like this:

- Review achievements for the rating period. Compliment the employee re these specific items: (1), (2), (3), etc.

- Find out if employee believes there are any problems that he/she is facing where I can help. Probe for specifics.

- Indicate areas where improvement is required or expected, explain why, and seek agreement.

- Summarize major points of discussion and find out if employee has anything else to add.

A third example: Suppose a manager is planning to attend a conference given by an outside organization. How does he or she prepare for this experience? Just go, listen to the speaker(s), ask a few questions along the way, then return to the job? Or should there be a game plan that assures that the manager will get the most from what is heard and seen?

All three of the former examples illustrate that when a manager has a systematic plan for communicating, he'll know what to listen for. When the antenna is up, and the manager is prepared to listen, he's in control of the communications process.

Benefits From Setting Listening Objectives

Managers help themselves be positive listeners by preparing a listening guide each time a meeting is attended or a pre-planned discussion with an employee is held. To explore this further, go back to the "conference" example just given. Suppose you are a sales manager attending a meeting in your organization where a new product is being introduced. You would be wise to develop listening strategies based on your objectives for going to the session. It's an advantage, a leg up. Your listening guide might look something like this:

These are some of the typical questions a sales manager might have that would need answers. While note-taking— keyed in to obtain responses to these questions—he'd be certain to jot down information on each of these items. Then, at the session, or when transcribing from his notes later, fill in the "Results" section and the "Follow-through" section. To demonstrate the value of doing this, see Exhibit 4B.

Also, the sales manager, before attending the conference, could phone or write the session presenter in his organization expressing interest in having the above points covered at the conference.

With your job duties from a listening standpoint already identified (Chapter One), you'd do well to consider preparing listening guides for each point whenever they are appropriate.

EXHIBIT 4A

Pre-Conference Listening Guide

Listening Objectives	Results	Follow-through
How will this product add to the profitability of my office?		
How will my salespersons benefit? Specifically, what will be the commission pay-out?		
What training will my staff need? When will it be given? How long will it take? Who will give it and where?		
Should I consider appointing a special sales coordinator for the product? Now? Later?		

LISTENING AND NOTE-TAKING

When listening to others we must be perceptive and prepared to understand the message in a single hearing. It's not like reading, where you can go back and make another pass at the printed page. Of course you could record a message or presentation on audio tape and listen to it later. That has its advantages and disadvantages, which will be discussed later. In face-to-face discussion or on the telephone, you may, on occasion, say something like "Would you repeat that? I'm not quite certain I understood what you said." when a difficult or confusing concept or idea is presented. You may

EXHIBIT 4B

Post Conference Report

Listening Objectives	Results	Follow-through
How will this product add to the profitability of my office?	Expect (shoot for) 5 percent profit rise in first year.	Review progress on quarterly basis
How will my salespersons benefit? Specifically, what will be the commission payout?	40 percent payout.	Develop strategy for marketing targets at next sales meeting.
What training will my staff need? When will it be given? How long will it take? Who will give it and where?	Dan Jones from home office will give instruction on (date and time) in our conference room.	Notify staff. Be sure prepared materials, if any, are distributed in advance and read.
Should I consider appointing a special sales coordinator for the product? Now? Later?	This needs more time to consider. Talk it over with senior salespeople.	

even question the speaker in a slightly different way by paraphrasing what was said or repeating a specific thought, then asking for clarification. It might go something like this: "You said the shipment will be packaged according to the desired specifications, but I don't recall you mentioning the delivery dates." It may be that the dates were given and you don't recall having heard them, or they were omitted and you're asking for additional input. Generally, though, out of sheer courtesy to the speaker, we're reluctant to interrupt or can't interrupt (particularly in the case of a platform presentation where the speaker has indicated that questions and comments will be fielded at the end of the session).

The ear is a primary source for sending messages to the brain. Our knowledge of the language, the subject, the speaker's attitude, our needs for selected information are compensating factors in helping us understand what is being said. Yet we know that retention in listening is difficult.

A resource for improving retention, as well as organizing ideas and information, is *note-taking*. In fact, your adeptness at getting main ideas down on paper in a succinct form may make a substantial difference in how much is retained. Your ability to get things down on paper in a desirable format and in a relevant form may be helped along when a speaker aids the listening process by arousing your interest in the subject and keeping your attention, but that is something you can't always anticipate.

A manager needs a structured method of taking notes, similar to the one below, that helps him/her listen for meaning and record central ideas.

Sales managers listening to a person give a practical demonstration of how to sell a particular product would do well to discipline their intake of ideas and information by taking notes in this fashion. The headings for recording pertinent items may differ based on the situation, e.g., a formal stand-up presentation vs. an informal discussion with someone. Nevertheless, the manager listens for key thoughts/concepts and records these in a succinct form for ready reference. In this way the notes are purposeful and relevant to the manager's needs.

EXHIBIT 4C

Main Idea	What is the speaker's major point?
Benefit to Me	How does the speaker's point of view affect me? What will it do for me?
Supporting Evidence/ Additional Ideas	What does the speaker say that substantiates his/her viewpoint? How am I convinced?
Action I Should Take	Now that I'm convinced this was worth my time and energy, here's what I should do. What do I have to do to get the benefits?

So far we've emphasized how to listen for meaning and detect central ideas. It is also important to resist biases, defuse emotions, and overcome distractions.

HOW TO RESIST BIASES, DEFUSE EMOTIONS, AND OVERCOME DISTRACTIONS

Listeners sometimes find that biases or prejudices (their own or someone else's) interfere with their ability to listen. I once asked a student of mine who was looking for sales motivational ideas to attend a lecture given by a prominent authority. When I asked her how the session had been of benefit she replied, "The speaker was a chauvinist; he spoke about salespeople as 'sales*men*.'" She found that an affront. Later she confided in me that it had been such a sore point it made her angry. As she listened she kept thinking about what she'd like to say to the speaker about her feelings.

True, the speaker's bias was unfortunate, but as a listener the student had to learn to overcome these feelings or be trapped into preoccupation with things that were far away from the speaker's main idea.

Our feelings about things often are strong, either in favor of something or opposed to something. We'd all be rather colorless automatons if this were not so. Yet in the most practical sense, particularly in business where teamwork and solidarity are vital to individual and organizational success, managers cannot afford to nurture biases or give vent to emotional outbursts.

Earlier, trigger words were identified as listening inhibitors. Certain words or ideas make us angry and get our dander up. The student who attended the sales lecture was prejudiced against the use of the word "men" as a way of identifying *all* salespeople. It made her so emotional, she blocked out the main ideas expressed by the speaker. The best thing to do to control emotions is to check them at the door. Easier said than done? Yes! It does take a special effort to make the controls work. Your best defense is to be aware of what might set you off. Reactions to emotionally charged words often give way to overt emotional responses. In some cases we may not say anything directly to the person who has aroused us. Nevertheless, as much as we may think we can hide or camouflage our reactions, something slips through. A frown, a fixed stare, dead silence—these are some of the giveaways. Once these subtle or not so subtle reactions are interpreted by the other person—whether correctly or incorrectly—the listening process suffers and the communication is weakened. Managers must make every effort to get emotions under control through their consciousness of what gets them aroused in the first place. The preventive act then becomes easier because you are prepared to keep the communication progressing in an orderly way.

Managers who've analyzed and learned to deal with distractions as barriers to listening often build up a high tolerance level for things that most other people have trouble dealing with. As a result, while conversing with someone they can safely ignore loud noises, persons interrupting, etc. However, what the manager cannot forget is that what may have been a distraction for him or her earlier and is now under control may be a distraction to the person with whom the manager is speaking. If listening is impaired on either side, the difficulties mount and the communications process suffers.

Managers set upon controlling their ability to listen must also be respectful of what may or may not prove a distraction to the other person. Therefore, they take steps to arrange facilities or circumstances in such a way that interference with listening can be avoided. However, once a distraction of any kind is so severe that it blocks or distorts the listening process, they have sense enough to do something to alleviate the situation. Sometimes a few reassuring words that convince the other person that listening is still taking place are sufficient. In more extreme cases it may be best to temporarily postpone a discussion, move to a different area, or take steps to eliminate the impingement.

The control factor is the principal battler against the takeover of anything that gets in the way of listening. When you made a list of barriers that impede listening you attacked each one in a positive way, saying in effect "I will find ways to eliminate or reduce the negative effect of this barrier."

The primary control is your *purpose* for listening. When your purpose is strong, you'll recognize the need to:

• Set listening objectives that help you listen for meaning and detect central ideas.

- Develop listening guides that fit your objectives whether you are attending meetings or having a preplanned discussion.

- Make notes that summarize the main content of the message and help you decide what to do next.

- Resist biases that contribute to distortions of communications.

- Defuse emotions that inhibit one's ability to think clearly.

- Eliminate, or at least tolerate, distractions that interfere with concentration.

5

GETTING THROUGH
TO OTHERS

Chapter 5 goals:

Describe how unspoken communications influence what you hear and what you say; explore how to organize thoughts into words that get messages across; identify how you guide and control feedback in order to assure and confirm that messages are understood.

Traditionally, listening has been thought of as a passive process in which a manager tunes in to what is heard and reacts accordingly. However, we've seen how a manager can develop skills and habits that make him or her a better processor of information and ideas. In effect, the manager is one who knows how to listen to what others say or do. Active listening takes place because the manager:

- Is committed to results.

- Appreciates that listening to others is a fundamental part of the job.

- Knows the requirements for being an effective listener and practices these 100 percent of the time.

The emphasis so far has been on how the manager responds to what is heard, the implication being that there are certain times when the manager has little or no control over what he or she listens to. Some representative examples are:

- Attending a lecture where the manager had no prior influence on the speaker's presentation.

- An executive (boss) calls a manager into the office and says, "Here are the things I'd like you to do to help us prepare for our production meeting next week."

Questions or comments may be made afterward that may change or influence what was said but the manager had little or no input at the time listening took place.

These are not uncommon situations in business. Yet of much greater commonality are those instances in which the manager has direct influence over the communications exchange. When a manager speaks with a prospect, a customer, a vendor, an employee, or others in the organization, whether in person or by phone, he is able to exercise certain controls over the listening process. The discussion can be kept on target through the use of probes: main points of agreement and disagreement can be crystallized and clarified; messages can be adjusted as attitudes, disposition, and acceptance or nonacceptance of ideas and information are uncovered through interpretation of nonverbal clues. The feedback, generated by the give and take of these exchanges, provides the direction so essential to managing the communication, and helps the manager do a more effective job of managing work and people.

In nearly every face-to-face situation in which a problem is discussed, a manager coaches a subordinate, discusses items with a peer, or talks with a boss about operational matters and other subjects, the manager is in a position to control the listening process. This occurs through the interpretation of unspoken communications on the parts of both the sender and receiver of a message and the ways a manager guides oral feedback in order to assure that messages are understood.

BODY LANGUAGE TO SUPPORT AND ENHANCE COMMUNICATION

A nonverbal communication is one that is not spoken. When we communicate, our nonverbal range is enormously encompassing, involving just about every aspect of the bodily mechanism. Nonverbals may seem complicated at times simply because people tend to interpret them differently in light of their own experiences, the feelings they have about the person speaking, the mood of the moment, etc. A smile from someone may be accepted as an expression of friendliness and warmth on one occasion, yet at another time, under different circumstances, it might be considered evidence of someone's smugness or derision. The act of looking away at a given point in a discussion may be open to all kinds of interpretations. To the speaker it may seem like an innocuous action having little or no relevance to what is being said; to the listener it may be looked upon quite differently.

We can be extremely conscious of how our nonverbals support or complement what we're saying. The words "I really do understand how you feel" when accompanied by a compassionate look and perhaps a gentle touch of the hand may make the message that much more believable and convincing. We can also be unaware or indifferent to the way our unspoken communication contradicts or negates what we say. Oftentimes our preoccupation with private thoughts may make us unaware that we are physically doing something that overrides our verbal message. For example, a manager invites an employee to enter his office to discuss a problem that the employee wishes to present. In the greeting the manager says, "Come in, Sally, have a seat. I've got plenty of time so tell me what's on your mind." Meanwhile, throughout the discussion, the manager keeps looking at his watch, thereby signaling to the employee that he has some place else to go or something else to do and wishes the employee would finish so he could move on. More than likely the employee will interpret the action negatively. Feeling uncomfortable, the employee may stop talking altogether, might become antagonistic, and/or assume the manager is not listening anyway. All of us probably have instant recall of many similar situations from our own experiences. There is no doubt that managers must be totally aware of the insistent power of unspoken messages.

The Spoken Word and Eye Contact

A management executive with whom I worked several years ago was considered a highly persuasive communicator. His physical presence (he wasn't a particularly tall or large man, but he carried himself well) commanded respect. While addressing a group of young, aggressive sales trainees he took a few moments to walk to the window where he looked out at the landscape. He stood there motionless for what was probably twenty seconds, but it seemed like a much longer time. He seemed to be contemplating important thoughts. Then he walked back to the front of the room and looked out at his audience, taking in everyone in one fixed glance. All eyes were focused on him and all ears were ready to tune in to his words. His next statement had a resounding effect on the group. The words he uttered immediately following this period of silence were accepted as gospel. The effect, of course, was devastating.

Certainly this kind of approach to gain the listener's attention may be calculated, deliberate, and oft-times transparent, the pyrotechnics interesting, even flamboyant. The important thing is that the message was heard because the listeners were really listening.

The fact that the speaker looked away, and then without speaking looked in this dramatic fashion again at everyone in the audience, illustrates how eye contact helps listeners pay attention.

Courses on presentation skills emphasize how to use eye contact so that listeners will be alert to what the speaker is saying and doing. Those who take these training classes learn to involve their audiences as active listeners by focusing on each person for specific periods of time, the theory being that when your eyes meet those of another, the listener gains reassurance that the speaker, although addressing a group, is speaking to him/her personally.

Eye contact in one-on-one situations is particularly supportive of the listening process. Here is where nonverbals play such an important role. The manager picks up nuances of behavior that might otherwise go unnoticed. More important, the manager helps the employee, client, or whoever he's speaking with focus on the subject at hand by merely reassuring, without words, that there is genuine interest in the person and in what he or she is saying.

Managers who do not set listening objectives often fall victim to inadvertently or indifferently doing things that discourage listener participation. Should a discussion seem to be heading nowhere, the manager may rivet attention on an object on the desk or continually twirl a pencil or pen in hand. This is not only distracting to the other person, but becomes a clear indication that the manager is disconcerted.

Eye contact also helps managers discern hidden messages. Fidgeting in one's chair, for instance, may be an indication that the chair itself is uncomfortable or perhaps has been sat in for too long a period. It also may show that the person is ill at ease over something else relevant or not relevant to the discussion.

Managers who keep their antennae up are sensitive to such occurrences. They appreciate how nonverbals support and complement the spoken message. They also understand that nonverbals provide clues to how people feel about themselves, the manager, and the situation at hand. These clues enable managers to adjust the spoken message or alter their body language to keep the focus on the results they are seeking.

THE SPOKEN WORD AND CHOICE OF LANGUAGE

Managers who are sensitive to how they listen and how others listen to them organize their ideas into words that get messages across. It's purely a matter of keeping things simple and to the point. Here's an example to illustrate how sentence structure alone can either distort or enhance meaning: "It is necessary that approval be given this proposal by Mr. Jones." If the manager who made this statement had chosen another, preferable way of expressing this thought, she might have said "Mr. Jones must approve this proposal." The latter statement has an action quality, whereas the former statement is passive and also open to another interpretation. The listener might think that it is Mr. Jones's proposal that requires approval.

Managers use vocabulary that fits within the listener's frame of reference and, at the same time, makes meaning clear. Embellishments (fancy words) often sound pompous and condescending. They add nothing to the conversation and frequently detract from the real intent of the message. For instance, if someone said "We seemed to be beset by a period of inclement weather for the past five days." the meaning might be understood, but think how much more forcefully the same thought comes across when someone says "It rained like hell for five straight days." It isn't just a case of using colorful language to keep the listener's attention, it's a matter of being aware of who you are speaking with and what will be most convincing to your audience.

Sometimes a word or two is used that may have a double meaning to the listener or provoke a negative feeling or reaction. When addressing a group, for example, saying "you people" tends to give listeners the impression that they are being lumped together in the speaker's mind as one big herd. It's a listener's turnoff and should be avoided. Skilled listeners will concentrate on the essential elements of the message, yet when you are the speaker it's inaccurate to assume that everyone is a skilled listener and allow yourself to fall into such traps.

Fortunately, listeners usually react to language via unspoken communications (a frown, looking down or away, a nod of the head in agreement or disagreement, a smile, etc.) or they may be straightforward in words by saying they approve or disapprove of what was said. However, it is well to remember that when language distorts or clouds meaning, listeners don't always reveal their feelings or objections either in words or through nonverbals. The effect of what was said is the same though; therefore, it could interfere with listening.

Certain words are accepted by some persons and rejected by others. Managers who are *positive listeners* steer clear of so-called trigger words which may set off negative reactions. Yet when the shoe is on the other foot and the other person says something that stimulates a negative reaction from the manager, the manager must be prepared to deal with his or her own feelings in a way that will not inhibit the progress of the communication. What's essential for the manager to keep in mind is that what is said—the choice of words to express meaning and how it is said—the use of the voice (vocal intonation, inflection, tempo, etc.) helps the other person sustain interest in listening. It also places the emphasis on getting the most out of the communication.

PROBING AS AN INFORMATION GATHERING TOOL

Perceptive managers are also skilled in keeping the listener's attention and interest by asking questions that direct or redirect the conversation toward the main purpose. The types of questions, and the manner in which they are asked, assure the other person that their participation is essential for resolving issues and seeking agreement. This questioning technique is called *probing*.

Probing is the manager's primary information-gathering tool. By asking questions in an orderly and progressive fashion, the manager gets input on the subject and learns more about the person. Probing also stimulates interest. The other person becomes more involved in the discussion because the probes help generate receptivity. Barriers that often get in the way of listening are broken down or dispelled because the other person is more relaxed, less likely to feel intimidated or fearful.

Normally, each probe given by the manager will get some kind of response. Generally, it will be an oral response, but it could also be nonverbal—some sort of physical reaction that indicates how the person feels about the question. Listening takes place when both persons are committed to the exchange; probing conditions this involvement. Probing makes the other person want to communicate and keeps the dialogue on track. Since probes are successive—one logically follows the other based on the ideas and information exchanged—the manager and the other person each have an obligation to listen. The manager chooses the type of probe that will give him or her the kinds of information sought.

What are the Various Types of Probes Managers Use?

The type of probe that gets the other person talking about the subject and themselves is called an *open probe*. Its very name implies that the respondent is given considerable freedom in choosing the type of response. Short, precise responses are untypical of open probes. Their purpose is to get the other person to "open up," to speak about experiences, feelings, ideas in such a way that the prober can get a broad idea of how the person thinks or feels about something. Examples of open probes:

- What do you think we should do about enforcing the new overtime policy?

- Give me your feelings about why you believe the plant personnel will have problems with the new equipment.

- If you don't think the first way will work, how would you do it?

Open probes force the other person to express how they feel about something, as well as think through (usually aloud) what they are saying. They help reinforce listening on a number of levels. Primary among these is that *open probes* show the other person that you have an interest in what they think. In contrast, if a manager were to say "I believe we should stop payment immediately. What do you think?" he or she might give a slightly colored response that indicates their caution in possibly disagreeing with the manager's point of view. Had the manager said, instead, "What do you think we should do about Mrs. Jones's account?" the respondent is likely to give an unbiased response because there's no subjective thought introduced that might distort the person's own thinking on the matter.

Neutral probes ask for additional information. They usually follow closely what the person has already stated about the subject. Example: "That sounds fine! What else do you think we should do?" When these probes follow a temporary pause or silence they are used to rekindle the discussion and assure the person you are interested in what he or she thinks.

Pauses naturally occur during a discussion. When the manager pauses deliberately it is usually to give the other person a chance to think through something. Often a pause at a given moment (a right moment) will indicate to the other person that they are not being forced to respond. The manager may use the pause to wait a moment before continuing the same subject or he or she may move on to something else.

Closed probes restrict the type of response—for instance where "yes" or "no" responses or short answers to questions are sought. Examples: "Who do you think should get the assignment, Finchley or Schultz?"; "Should we go down to the plant tomorrow at 10 A.M.?"

Fact-finding questions typically fit into the closed-probe category. "What time did you start work at your previous job?" would be representative of this kind of probe. Too many of these in succession may intimidate the other person. They should be used sparingly to obtain precise responses.

Rhetorical questions generally have built-in answers. They are put in such a way that one couldn't possibly answer any differently than the implied, acceptable response. Example: "You wouldn't throw good money away, would you?" Their purposes are limited and managers should use them carefully. What they do is assure the other person that a point of view has been substantiated.

Summary statements, on the other hand, assure the other person that the manager has been listening. The manager summarizes information or a series of ideas that were expressed. Example: "Let's see if I understood what you told me — you showed Mary the new procedure, found out there were some kinks, then spoke with the foreman." Summary statements also make certain that the manager has gotten the information correct in the first place.

Reflective questions or statements feed back or repeat what has been said. Example:

Supervisor: "I don't know. Somehow I just can't seem to get started on the report."

Manager: "Get started . . . ?"

Supervisor: "Yes . . . I mean every time I start writing down ideas I begin thinking there's more to be done. . . . I hesitate to put my ideas into words.

Reflective questions help show that the manager is listening and understands. They also promote further elaboration by the other person.

Often, reflective questions enable the manager to indicate support for the person, lend encouragement, or compliment the person on something done or said. For example, after the supervisor (above) made his last comment, the manager might reply:

Manager: "Yes, I know how you feel. It's happened to me too. Look at it this way. When we're concerned about doing a job well, we seldom think we're ready to put it all down in words. But that shouldn't stop us from trying. . . . What do you think?

When probes are used intelligently they are one of the most valuable tools a manager has at his disposal to ensure understanding and reach agreement. They are critical to the listening process at all times when two or more persons are engaged in any kind of discussion or dialogue.

What Probing Really Accomplishes

It is the manager's commitment to achieve results that is the prime motivator in the development of useful listening skills and habits. Probing is one of the primary means for seeking out all necessary facts, ideas, and information. In addition, the intelligent use of probes assures those in authority with whom the manager has regular contact that there is personal concern for performing one's job to the best of one's ability. Prospects, customers, and vendors view the treatment they receive as evidence of the manager's concern for their needs and interests. Subordinates, on the other hand, because they usually have the most frequent contact with the manager, accept probes as a natural part of their communication with the manager. In fact, they may be likely to emulate the manager's performance to such an extent that

EXHIBIT 5A

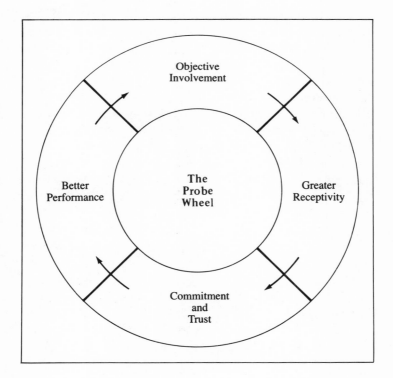

Source: Listening: A Guide to Effective Communications Management. A Warren
H. Reed, Consultants course.

they become proficient at using probes without necessarily being trained to do so.

The *probe wheel*, Exhibit 5A, illustrates the linking process that evolves when managers use probes effectively.

The first part of the cycle—*objective involvement*—refers to the manager's concern for all aspects of the job. It not only refers to his/her ability to plan, organize, direct, control, and evaluate, but the way the human elements are handled—showing respect for another's point of view; having empathy toward someone else's outlook. Probes promote *objective involvement*, both on the part of the manager who successfully uses them to initiate and sustain productive discussions, but also on the part of persons inside and outside the organization. As a result, there is *greater receptivity* to ideas. This occurs because employees and others appreciate the manager's outlook and find his/her behavior supportive of their needs. As the manager learns to listen effectively through intelligent probing, he gets positive input from others. The constructive ideas and information he gets enable him to do his job more effectively, leading to *commitment and trust*. The end result is *better performance* all around. Because persons perform well, the cycle continues. By feeling good about what one accomplishes and seeing that what one does is appreciated, *objective involvement* remains a constant and so the cycle is continuous. Probes are, indeed, a special force that promote listening and add to the manager's total effectiveness.

PUTTING PROBES
TO WORK

Chapter 6 goals:

To demonstrate that the intelligent use of probes—whether planned or spontaneous—helps the manager get results in a variety of common business situations.

In Chapter Five probes were identified as that "special force that promotes listening and adds to the manager's total effectiveness." Managers use probes in almost every form of oral communication; however, probes that get the best results are those that help obtain the desired response while, at the same time, supporting the listening process.

Putting probes to work to elicit responses that keep discussions focused on obtaining the desired results require that the manager carefully select the most appropriate kinds of probes. Each probe should be as relevant as possible to what the manager needs to know and be consistent with the developmental pattern of the discussion. Listening always requires concentration; therefore, it is easier to listen well and, in turn, contribute positively to the discussion when the probes support the logical flow of conversation. For example, when interviewing a job applicant a manager or interviewer would be expected at the outset of the discussion to ask questions that help put the applicant at ease. Even when applicants show few visible signs of apprehension about the interview, it is safe to assume that they are seldom completely at ease. When probes help applicants feel comfortable and relaxed they listen better and speak more freely.

Selection of the best type of probe is also important. In order to confirm how long a person worked at a previous job and learn what positions were held during that period, a *closed* probe and *fact-finding* probe would be acceptable and expected. For example:

> *Closed Probe.* I see from your employment application that you worked at XYZ Company for six years. Is that correct? (Applicant's response: "Yes.")

> *Fact-finding Probe.* What positions did you hold during that time? (Applicant goes on to name the positions held.)

It is logical now for the manager to proceed to probe for specific information about the applicant's experience and attitudes toward his or her previous work. The probing is progressive, with a constant building of information that is related to the manager's objective: "Find the most qualified person for the current opening."

What the manager listens to is directly proportional in quality to the types of questions directed to the applicant. A disorganized, undisciplined interviewer will allow an applicant to ramble. With little or no attempt to control the feedback initially, the sketchy and disjointed input from the applicant doesn't provide the manager with much to go on. What the manager listens to, in such circumstances, is what the applicant wants him to hear, not what the manager needs to know. Yet, when forthright and insightful planning are part of a manager's approach, there is a much greater opportunity to get meaningful information. As a result there is a flow and continuity to the exchange that keeps the manager's objective up front and keeps his/her thinking on target. As rapport develops between the manager and the interviewee, listening on both their parts is enhanced.

The manager who plans to control the interview and seek the most qualified applicant might organize his plan as illustrated in Exhibit 6A. The real test of the manager's ability to communicate effectively centers around the feedback he gets from the applicant. If we examine the interview process closely, it is during the "conducting" portion that the manager receives the kind of information that enables him or her to make an accurate assessment of the candidate's qualifications. Here the well-organized manager who wants to control the interview develops speaking patterns that promote listening. Tone of voice, pace of delivery, and choice of language (vocabulary, phrasing, etc.) all blend together to stimulate receptivity. Managers, by definition, are expected to carry the ball in most verbal exchanges. Applicants for positions, however, may also preplan for their interview and come with certain inquiries about the job, the company, the department, the people that they intend to ask somewhere along the line. The manager should anticipate that these questions need to be asked and provide opportunities during the discussion for the applicant to raise them.

HOW PROBES ARE USED IN JOB APPLICANT INTERVIEWS

To illustrate how probes can be used in a job applicant interview situation, examine Exhibit 6B. Note that the five

EXHIBIT 6A

The Employment Interview

PREPARING (what you have to know and do)
1. Know job (what to do)
2. Know job standards (how well job should be done)
3. Know salary range
4. Know job qualifications: experience; skills
5. Know EEO requirements
6. Arrange time and place
7. Review application/résumé

CONDUCTING (control, guide, assess)
1. Greet applicant; set climate
2. Obtain information: education, prior work experience, skills
   —Use probes to obtain this information
   —Appraise information as it relates to job
   —Take notes
3. Give information
   —Describe the job; relate to applicant's background
   —Answer questions/comments
4. Summarize results of interview
5. Close

DECIDING (weigh key factors; make decision)
1. Evaluate all relevant data (be wary of personal bias)
2. Make decision
3. Communicate with applicant
   —If no, thank and wish well
   —If yes, decide if second interview needed; get details settled (start date, salary, etc.)

---

types of probes that are most frequently used during the interview are:

Open

Neutral

Fact-finding

Pause/Silence

Summary

Managers who plan each interview following the suggested approach shown in Exhibit 6A will write down selected probes that they may wish to use during the interview. In this way they will not overlook listening for critical information that helps them make their final decision. They are also aware of the advantages of eye contact for noting observable behavior. The nonverbal clues exhibited by the applicant are of equal importance in the listening process.

It is time to focus attention on some other types of formal and informal communications in which managers can use probes to promote listening and get the results they want, namely:

• Conducting performance appraisal interviews

• Delegating work assignments and projects

• Training employees

• Coaching

• Counseling

• Prospecting

• Selling clients a product or service

EXHIBIT 6B

Successful Probing Techniques for the Interviewer

Type of Probe	Purpose	Example
OPEN	Used to stimulate thinking and get the applicant talking.	Tell me what you liked about your last job.
NEUTRAL	Encourages interviewee to elaborate on a topic being discussed.	I see . . . go on. What else can you tell me?
FACT-FINDING	Used to get a short, precise response or seek specific data.	What hour did you start work at your previous job? Why did you leave your last position?
PAUSE/ SILENCE	Allows the interviewer and the interviewee time to collect thoughts or reflect on what's been said.	
SUMMARY	Summarizes information and a series of ideas that were expressed.	Let's see if I understand what you told me. . . . You worked on your last job for five years, then decided to try a new career.

In each of the above types of communication it is important for the manager to determine his objectives. It is too easy to lose control of the discussion and thereby make listening an academic exercise when the purpose is not clear in the manager's mind. The manager who is an effective listener uses probes to direct discussions toward achieving the objectives.

Specific objectives in any communication may differ based on the circumstances in a given situation and the kinds of persons with whom the manager is interfacing. However, overriding objectives tend to remain fairly constant. For instance, here are common objectives related to the topics shown above:

Interviewing Job Applicants
Select the most qualified person for a specific job.

Conducting Performance Appraisal Interviews
Motivate employees to achieve better performance.

Delegating Work Assignments and Projects
One or more of the following are common objectives:
Broaden the experience of an employee.
Test his/her ability to perform a certain task.
Relieve the manager of doing a nonpriority task.
Meet a critical time deadline.

Training Employees
Ensure that standards of performance quality and quantity are met by teaching employee job fundamentals.

Coaching
Follow through on the effectiveness of the training given on and off the job.

Counseling
Guide an employee toward the solution of a problem

(work related or nonwork related) that is affecting performance.

Prospecting
Develop new business that will increase sales.

Selling Clients a Product or Service
Maintain positive client relationships and increase sales volume.

THE PERFORMANCE APPRAISAL INTERVIEW

Preliminaries to Conducting the Interview

Companies, and their respective departments, normally have standard practices for appraising employee performance. This means managers are familiar with the appraisal process: the forms and documentation required; the frequency with which appraisals are written and submitted to the human-resource group or others in the organization; the requirements for holding a formal performance review session with an employee.

Managers who see the value in communicating performance results will have specific documentation in each employee's file containing information about the employee's achievements, as well as notations about any deficiencies in performance. During the course of business over the appraisal period the manager will keep the employee informed about the quality of his/her performance, identifying the successes, complimenting the employee for any achievements and special effort, and coaching in areas that need improvement. When this is done the interview becomes a summing up of the employee's current performance status—

there are no surprises—and permits the discussion to center on the real objective: "motivating the employee to achieve better performance."

Thus, the interview becomes the manager's tool for communicating his/her interest in the employee. During the period of the interview the employee is given ample opportunity to comment on his/her own view of what has been accomplished and to make suggestions for further improvement. Employees who are committed to teamwork because they work with a results-oriented manager and see the manager as a supporter give ideas freely that also help improve the department's overall operation. In their book *Improving Productivity Through People*,[1] the authors indicate that "a performance appraisal can be thought of as a 'productivity audit,' in which a 'balance sheet' on the subordinate's performance is drawn up, his 'net worth' to the organization is calculated, and plans for 'increasing his net worth' in the next auditing period are made." When managers keep this in mind they'll plan their interviews carefully so that employees are aware of what they've accomplished, know where improvement is warranted, and explore directions that might be taken to ensure success.

Planning the Appraisal Interview

After completing the performance appraisal document, the manager plans the interview. The document serves as the chief reference source for discussing specific elements of performance. Motivating the employee to achieve better performance is a realistic objective for the interview, and the manager makes this a primary element of the ensuing discussion with the employee. He also considers the benefits of the interview from his point of view and from the employee's outlook. These benefits include:

- Clearly identifying what is expected in the way of performance.

- Letting the employee know where he stands—identifying and evaluating overall strengths and areas for improvement.

- Establishing short- and/or long-term job goals.

- Identifying potential for promotion.

- Preparing the employee for advancement, coaching, and training.

The approach to the interview will depend on a number of factors:

- *The length of time the manager and employee have worked together.* Is either one or both new to the department? Is this the first formal appraisal session?

- *The current working relationship between manager and employee.* Is rapport good? Is the employee a self-starter or in need of guidance and direction? Has the employee been receptive to criticism of performance in the past?

- *The policies of the firm concerning the evaluation process and procedure.*

- *The manager's objective assessment of the employee's potential for development and promotion.* Is there room for advancement in the department? Does the employee's current performance show potential for growth?

Managers are wise to beware of making definitive value judgments about the employee's capacity for achievement before conducting the interview. Most managers learn from experience that the interview itself can be an eye-opener. It is the ideal time to acquire new evidence about the employee's goals, needs, attitudes toward the job, and interest in self-development.

LISTENING AND PERFORMANCE APPRAISALS

Listening at performance appraisal sessions is critical to both the manager and the employee. Generally, the employee wants to know where he or she stands in the manager's eyes; the manager wishes to give the employee an objective evaluation of his or her contributions, as well as create a climate where the employee will participate willingly in the work effort and take a personal interest in his own self-development.

Interviews that fail—where the employee is left unmotivated and even disenchanted—are those where the manager does most of the talking and little, if any, listening. Managers who say, in effect, "Now let me tell you what the company expects..." sound as if they are lecturing, not communicating. An employee's negative response to this kind of treatment will stymie the manager's future efforts to turn things around. Managers must remember that employees listen when they know the manager sees things from their (the employee's) perspective.

The most successful appraisal interviews are those in which the manager and the employee have already set targets for effective performance. The appraisal time then becomes a summing-up and measurement of progress before a plan to begin a new series of agreed-upon objectives is begun.

Excluding jobs where the routines are seldom altered, this approach is very useful.

How Probes Help Performance Appraisals

It is impractical to attempt to provide a list of "ideal" probes for conducting an effective appraisal interview. Too many factors are involved: the type of job; company policies; the working relationship between manager and employee, etc. As already discussed, however, probes normally stimulate the listening process when they are purposefully selected to meet the discussion objective. Therefore, managers may wish to make their own choices from the following examples:

> What do you believe have been your most significant contributions to the department over the course of the past year?

> How can I help you reach the goals you've identified for yourself?

> What other areas of work or jobs in the company do you believe you are most suited for?

> Why do you believe you've been successful at doing that type of task?

Open probes are useful in particular, since they encourage the employee to speak freely about his or her work. They also make it evident that the manager has empathy for the employee's sensitivity about the work.

DELEGATING WORK ASSIGNMENTS AND PROJECTS

One or more of the following are common objectives for delegating work assignments and projects:

Broaden the experience of the employee.

Test employee's ability to perform a certain task.

Relieve the manager of doing a nonpriority task.

Meet a certain time deadline.

Before the manager delegates, he must assess the employee's disposition toward performing work that is different or new. For instance, suppose the manager wants to test an employee's ability to perform a certain task. The manager may decide to do this because he feels the employee is ready to do more or because he wants to see if there's room for the employee to stretch beyond current capacities. Regardless of what the manager's motivation may be, he must first determine the employee's willingness to get involved in the assignment. The manager might learn about the employee's attitude by probing in the following manner:

"Cynthia, I've been concerned about how effectively our salespeople are meeting production standards. For the past few months, Data Processing has been giving me tabulated reports on sales volume by person for each of our regional areas. Now I need to compile a report that compares each region's production. It will help me see where our salespeople are getting the job done and determine which areas need help. I could use your assistance in putting this together. Can you help me?"

In this short introduction to the task the manager has done three essential things:

- Given a general description of the nature of the task.

- Indicated the rationale for performing the work.

- Asked for the assistance of the employee.

By setting the stage in this manner the manager has deliberately used a sales technique that encourages the "client" to want to participate.

In no way does it guarantee an immediate positive response. If the employee has strong self-doubts about her ability to perform the work or feels unqualified to do it, the manager may encounter some reluctance or hesitation. However, by introducing the task in this way, the employee has the chance to:

- Show her interest in helping the manager.

- Ask questions about the specifics of the task.

As the manager observes the employee's nonverbal reactions and listens to the comments and questions raised about the project, he may follow through with clarifying information or, where necessary, use additional probes to counteract resistance and help persuade the employee that she will benefit from doing the task.

In contrast, the manager who is concerned primarily about getting the task done and less about the employee's level of interest or degree of confidence might introduce the task quite differently:

> "Cynthia, I'm compiling a report on sales production for each region. Here's what I want you to do to help me get it done. . . ."

When the manager resorts to this kind of "do it or else" approach and the employees resists, the manager is forced to defend his decision. As a result the manager may be faced with serious conflict that could have been avoided. Invitation always seems to work better than declaration.

Often, employees will indicate a willingness to do additional work by taking on duties without being asked or they may volunteer to do more. When this happens—and the manager is willing to delegate—he has a distinct advantage, but he also must be practical. Some employees are more than willing to take on delegated work, but may lack the required skills to do the job effectively. It is too easy and too dangerous to be overwhelmed by an employee's receptivity and merely give the project away. Instead, the manager must be prepared to train and coach sufficiently enough to get the task done properly. Probing helps the manager know how and when to proceed.

TRAINING EMPLOYEES

Over the years training-within-industry guidelines have been a consistent source of reference for managers in training employees to do their jobs. This is a four-step method that consists of the following elements:

Prepare Employee
Put at ease.
State job's purpose.
Check prior knowledge.
Create interest.
Arrange setting.

Teach Task
Tell/show—one step at a time.

Stress key points.
Use simple language.
Explain terminology.

Tryout Performance
Learner: Performs task.
Explains steps/key points.

Instructor: Corrects errors.
Encourages questions.
Instructs clearly, completely, patiently.

Follow-through
Put on own.
Tell who will help.
Check frequently.
Encourage questions.
Taper off coaching.

Before the training is given, the manager or his/her delegate designated to do the training must do the following:

Prepare and use job and task descriptions.
All major tasks related to the job are defined in sequential steps that advance the work, accompanied by explanatory key points that help the employee understand the step.

Design timetables for completing the training.
These timetables enable the manager to keep track of all training started and completed by employees.

Be ready to give the training.
Have all supplies, materials, equipment in place to administer training.

Arrange the work space.
The work space is organized the way the employee is expected to keep it on the job.

The types of probes that encourage trainee participation in the learning experience are:

Probe	Purpose	Example
Open	Used to stimulate thinking and get the trainee talking.	Why do you enter information on the log?
Neutral	Encourages trainee to elaborate on what is being learned.	I see ... go on. That's good ... and then
Pause	Allows trainee time to collect thoughts or reflect on what was said or done.	
Fact-finding	Used to get a short, precise response or seek specific data.	In which file do you place these reports?
Summary statements	Summarizes other person's thoughts, assures your understanding, and shows learner you were listening.	You've told me that after you complete the entries on this report you enter your signature and give the report to the section supervisor for approval.

Managers who do the actual training get the best results when they follow all of the aforementioned guidelines. When the training responsibility is delegated to others, as it is most often, the manager must be certain that the trainers know and practice instructional requirements.

One of the most important ingredients of the training is patience. The trainer must give a trainee ample time and encouragement to learn each task, providing the trainee with constant feedback on the progress of the learning.

The trainer's effective use of probes and ability to listen are two more vital elements of the total training process. Throughout the four-step method from "Prepare Employee" through "Follow-through" both the instructor and the trainee are active listeners. The trainee gets information in order to perform the tasks; the trainer gives instruction and obtains feedback on the learner's performance. The trainee does most of the listening during the "Teach Task" phase, the trainer during the "Tryout Performance" phase. A motto often used in training is "If the learner hasn't learned, the instructor hasn't taught." This is another way of saying "If the instructor hasn't probed for feedback, there's little guarantee that the learner can do the job."

COACHING

Once the fundamentals of the job are learned and the trainee meets the required standards for performing the work, the manager should be prepared to follow through by coaching on the job. Periodic checkups on performance tell the manager how successfully the employee is performing and provide opportunities to reinforce the learning.

Since certain elements of the job may not be performed as frequently as others, it is possible for the learner to forget what to do or be uncertain about each element of a task. One of the best ways for the manager to ensure that coaching is given when it is needed is to encourage the employee to let him know when additional training or assistance is needed. This fixes the responsibility for job guidance with the employee. It does not relieve the manager of the obligation to give the employee help when the manager believes it is required. Production or sales reports often are a reliable way of determining when coaching should be given, but the informal agreement between manager and employee that prompts the employee to volunteer for assistance makes the partnership work best.

Regular follow-through on performance may be a planned event, e.g., weekly meetings between the employee and the manager or his delegate to review progress. Or it could be impromptu, the manager stopping by at the employee's work area.

Where it is an informal follow-through, then probes such as "How are things coming along?" or when referring to a specific aspect of the work "Is _____ coming along all right?" might be typical. Where there are scheduled meetings on work progress, then the following approach might uncover any need for coaching: "Let's review what has been accomplished this week." The manager or the employee then indicates what has been done/accomplished. Based on the feedback, the manager might say "Regarding _____, why don't we review some of things that need to be done." The employee states what he knows about the task/item, and the manager directs questions that help assure him the employee can perform as required.

Managers who are sensitive to the need for employees to maintain control over the proprietorships of their jobs will use probes that help employees test their own knowledge. The probes will not only relate to *what* the person does or *how* a task is done, but to the reasons *why*. For example, when a sales manager coaches a salesperson he might say:

> "You indicated your goal for this year was to earn
> $_____. Your production after six months is $_____.
> That's pretty good, but as you can see, unless it increases by
> $_____ for the balance of the year, you may have trouble
> reaching this goal. What do you believe you need to do to
> make that happen?"

In this way the manager is fixing the responsibility for improved performance where it belongs—with the employee. The probes are not intimidating; they are supportive. In effect, the manager is saying "It's your goal, here's the latest status report on your progress, what can you do to help yourself?" Once the employee has responded to the original question—"What do you believe you need to do to make that happen [reach the goal]?"—the manager can offer assistance or guidance in helping the employee.

The manager may believe the salesperson needs to build production by making better use of a product in the line or by trying different prospecting methods. Whatever strategy the manager believes will help the employee, the employee must also believe it will work.

A series of probes, such as the following, may put the need/idea in perspective:

Manager: "Have you considered prospecting with persons who have real estate holdings?"

Employee: "Yes, but I've been concentrating on contacts with corporate executives in other industries."

Manager: "That's fine . . . and you've done well in those areas. But you ought to consider the good results you might get if you also checked out the real estate group."

Employee:	"Why do you think that's a good move?"
Manager:	"You know that extensive condominium construction going on in the west section of town?"
Employee:	"You mean the 'RightWay' project?"
Manager:	"Yes! You might check with the executive group at that realtor's office. Perhaps they'd be interested in what you could offer them in our product line. It might be a good way to increase your sales."
Employee:	"Hmmm!"
Manager:	"There's no guarantee that you'll click with them on the first contact. But it could be worth a try. I don't think anyone's gone after them yet. The income from this group could get you closer to your dollar goal either this month or next. Do you think it's worth a try?"

This type of probing goes on until at some point the salesperson agrees to try the recommended approach or perhaps comes up with another equally satisfactory prospecting plan of his/her own.

The critical element in coaching is to practice it regularly with all employees, regardless of their newness in the department or their relative status in performing the work. Probes either uncover needs or at least assure the manager that all is well. Listening is enhanced in all its aspects because employees know the manager cares about how they are performing and the manager knows he/she is on top of things.

COUNSELING

Counseling refers to a manager's efforts to assist an employee in resolving a problem that may or may not be work related. It differs from coaching in that coaching occurs as a natural follow-up on job performance, whereas counseling might occur at any time. Employees may come to the manager for help voluntarily, or the manager may learn through observation and discussion that the employee needs some kind of assistance. Quite often the root problem that precipitates the need for counseling is of a personal nature that has created tensions for the employee and influenced his behavior on the job.

Some types of clues that frequently indicate a counseling need are:

Absenteeism

Daydreaming/lack of concentration

Irritability

Work errors

Disagreements or arguments with other employees

Unless an employee volunteers information, it is often difficult to determine that counseling should be given. It is not easy for most employees to openly discuss things that cause them distress, either because they are embarrassed to admit they're having a problem or because they shy away from burdening the manager with personal matters.

Managers who have their antennae up seem to have a sixth sense about when to probe to uncover a counseling need. Through their sensitivity they're able to reassure employees that they are concerned about the person's welfare. Their initial probes help relieve the employee's anxiety about talking about sensitive subjects. The types of probes that are widely used have been identified earlier: Open, Neutral, Fact-finding, Pause/Silence, and Summary.

Managers do not pretend to be private counselors, dispensing advice freely on matters outside their realm of control or authority. Instead, they help guide the employee toward solving his or her own problem. They do this by proving that they have a genuine concern for the individual.

PROBING AS A PROSPECTING AND SELLING TECHNIQUE

Managers who have the responsibility for generating sales use probes extensively when speaking with prospective clients. Regardless of the method of contact (most often by telephone or in person), the manager follows a specific plan of action that includes the following elements:

- Determine sales dollar goal and/or new account goal for a specific period of time.

- Estimate how many new customers are needed to achieve this goal.

- Select target groups for sales contacts. Be prepared to qualify these contacts, i.e., determine that persons need and can afford the product or service.

- Know benefits and features of products and/or services thoroughly.

- Have a plan of action before making a call or presentation. Have questions to ask and be prepared to ask for the order or make a follow-through appointment. Stress benefits before features.

- Plan each day ahead of time and stick to the plan.

- Be persistent, but also be patient. It may take several contacts over a period of time to get an order or arrange an appointment.

- Take time to listen. Probe for information by asking questions that get the prospect talking. Expect to listen most of the time. Remember why people are willing to listen—because there's a benefit for them.

- Keep meticulous records on the prospect's interests, objectives, and record the outcomes of each contact.

- When a prospect says "no," find out why. Be prepared to break down resistance by probing. Have a list of typical, anticipated objections with suggested approaches for overcoming them.

- Ask for referrals, even when the order is not obtained.

- Don't lose sight of the purpose(s) for making each contact—open accounts/make sales.

Open probes are useful to get the person talking about needs and objectives. For instance, a sales manager making a prospecting call who represents a financial services organization might ask during the course of a conversation:

"Can you tell me what you do with your serious investment money?"

Closed probes may also be used:
"Have you ever used our product before?" If the response to this question was "yes," an Open probe might follow:

"Please tell me about your experience with it."

If the response had been "no," the manager might follow with a Fact-finding probe:

"What products are you using now?"

In effect, the sales manager has the option of using a wide variety of different types of probes to help him meet his call objectives. Normally, these objectives are:

- Introduce the product or service.

- Generate interest.

- Qualify the prospect.

- Overcome resistance.

- Handle objections.

- Make the sale or open the account.

- Set up appointments for future contacts.

The sales manager who plans his contacts in advance is prepared to deal with prospect resistance and handle the prospect's objections. This is done by making a list of anticipated prospect reactions to the probes the sales manager selects. These reactions include:

"I don't have the money right now."

"I don't have the time."

"I've used similar products or services before and I don't care for them."

"What can you offer me that someone else can't."

Each objection is looked upon as an opportunity to move toward the sales close. When the sales manager addresses the objection with facts and new information, the prospect can see more readily what the advantages are in using the product or service. Indeed, it is when objections are not uncovered through insightful probing that the manager may fail to reach the close or open the account.

The practice of phoning prospective customers to generate interest in products and services that lead to sales is known as telemarketing. The concept relies very heavily on the skills of the caller in using probes that work.

Dealing with customers is not much different, except that the basic need to buy a product or use a service has already been established. Needs and wants change, however, over a period of time as income may fluctuate and status requirements may alter. The manager must continue to probe to be certain the customer is getting what is wanted and is satisfied. This helps solidify the trust and commitment between both parties.

NOTES

[1]*Improving Productivity Through People Skills* by Robert E. Lefton, V. R. Buzzotta, and Manuel Sherberg, published by Ballinger Publishing Company, Cambridge, Mass., 1980.

LISTENING
ON THE TELEPHONE

Chapter 7 goals:

Describe how managers get desirable results from telephone communications when they: Develop a system for handling calls that enables them to concentrate on priority items and reduce interruptions and distractions; Use the voice to promote active listening.

CONTROLLING
THE TELEPHONE

Managers who decide to keep daily activity logs in order to improve their performance are often surprised to find they spend a considerable amount of time on the phone. Estimates range from 20 percent to as high as 50 percent of any given working day. Incoming calls, generally, outnumber outgoing calls by about five to one. The control of the phone so that listening time is devoted primarily to essential aspects of the work is critical to the manager's success. The well-organized manager designs, with the help of a secretary and staff, a regular strategy for handling incoming and outgoing calls.

Think carefully about your own situation. It is not only

a question of whether you listen well on the phone and are listened to by others; another issue that arises is: Should you be listening at all? This means that one of the first things a manager tackles is how and when to screen incoming calls so listening time is devoted to priority items. Yes, it is polite and often efficient to answer and place one's own calls. You have to decide whether or not you can accomplish what has to be done and still do this. From a practical standpoint, however, the manager needs some help in this area.

Screening Incoming Calls

It is natural to assume that people tend to want to listen on the phone when they receive a greeting that is warm and friendly, the kind of greeting in which the spoken words and the tone of voice are both cordial and businesslike. What are some of the ways that your secretary and staff can assist you in screening calls?

Watch One's Manners—Stay far away from offensive and unprofessional greetings. How do you feel when you place a call to someone and the voice on the line, usually unidentified, responds, "What is this in reference to?" Chances are you wouldn't greet someone at your office door with that kind of stilted, unfriendly comment. Better to say, "Mr. [the manager's name] is not available at the moment, is there anything I can do to help you [then state the caller's name, if it has been given]." Yet, some business persons fail to see how the initial greeting prepares the way for listening effectiveness. They falsely believe that the visual impact is missing—but it isn't missing. When the greeting is cold or officious we tend to envision a person who seems indifferent and callous. The objective should be to break down barriers to listening, not to create them. Then the emphasis will be placed correctly on fulfilling the purpose of the call rather than coping with side issues having to do with feelings of frustration.

Coaching the Staff on Telephone Practices—The wise manager sets up ground rules for handling the phone. He or she does this by first finding out what the staff believes should be done about the phone so that work priorities get preferential treatment. Employees will probably tell you that they can handle certain calls without having the calls come to you. By delegating certain tasks to them, calls related to these tasks will fall into their bailiwick naturally. Seek agreement on procedure with everyone, then follow through to be certain everything is done properly. Uniformity, with some degree of flexibility, is the best policy. What is important is to get a system going that works.

Your direct line, for instance, should be answered in a consistent manner. Example: "John Jones's office, Helene Spence." Also, when the manager answers a staff member's phone, the same efficient and courteous response should be given: "Helene Spence's office, John Jones." When it's a general line for the department, the preferred response would be to give the department name/title ("Sales Department"; "Production Department") and the name of the person answering.

What's also important is to consider the listening implications. When the greeting is acceptable a positive impression of your organization and your operation is formed. The impression usually sticks when the treatment is consistently professional. Receptionists, like switchboard attendants, present a front-line image to the public; therefore, it is essential that they project a warm, friendly, courteous manner on the phone (as well as in person). Since they must direct traffic and keep the flow of calls moving expeditiously to the right persons, this puts them in the best position to generate good feelings about the company. In a way they are the first "sales" contact an outsider has with anyone in the firm. It helps if they know something about your product or service, as well as who's who in the organization. This enables them to assist callers who may be uncertain about whom to talk with or which department to contact. When their response to a caller indicates that they have listened well and care, it helps that person feel receptive to whatever you may say later.

Never consider these things trivial or inconsequential. Just think of how you feel when you want to talk with someone on a matter of concern to you and are flatly put down or put off before you're able to get through.

Return Calls

One of your objectives should be to reduce substantially the number of calls you have to return. Your staff members will broaden their experience when you've delegated certain responsibilities to them that require that they follow through properly with the caller.

Outgoing Calls

Managers may prefer to place their own outgoing calls, with a few exceptions. For instance, the assistance of a secretary or an assistant may be needed to place the call when the manager is having a discussion with one or more persons and needs the input of someone else by phone. The immediate discussion can be continued while an employee attempts to reach the third party. When a manager places a call directly an acceptable way to make the contact is to say something like:

"This is John Jones of the Cambridge Company. May I speak with Ms. Aldridge?"

Don't be surprised if the person with whom you speak responds by saying:

"May I ask who's calling?"

It happens this way; it's frustrating, but a repeat of the identification in a pleasant tone may be necessary in such cases. Yes, it accentuates the listening deficiencies of untrained persons, but it's part of the real world. Just be sure that you and your staff don't let such things happen on your end. It's best to identify yourself in this way because the person you are speaking with is likely to ask who you are or want the name of your firm anyway. Give it to them up front and try to save yourself the time of repeating it later.

REDUCING INTERRUPTIONS AND DISTRACTIONS

Even when a manager is speaking on the telephone, employees and others are apt to interrupt or buzz the office on the intercom. Due to these interruptions, continuity in the phone discussion is often lost. When necessary interruptions occur that are brief and do not require hanging up the receiver, the manager should excuse himself/herself. Then, when returning to the phone, a polite "I'm sorry about that" followed by a short summary statement of the main points of the discussion up to that point help keep things on track. Since the slightest delay always seems interminable, it is easy for someone to lose the train of thought.

Managers can, however, eliminate or cut down interruptions by simply having it known that no interruptions may be tolerated that are not of an emergency nature. With proper screening of incoming calls, chances are the manager will not be interrupted except on urgent matters. An efficient secretary intercedes to help or promises that as soon as the manager's phone conversation or face-to-face discussion is ended the manager will do what is needed. Putting another call through and forcing the manager to try to balance two calls at once usually doesn't work too well. One or both persons may be shortchanged from the jumping back and forth, thereby jeopardizing listening effectiveness.

Normally, there's a temptation to move quickly to the more pressing of the two calls, with the result that the one that does not take precedence is abandoned abruptly. To ensure that the transition is accommodating to the person whose conversation is terminated, managers should do the following:

• Offer a satisfactory explanation for discontinuing the call, one that does not make the person feel like a second fiddle.

• Briefly summarize what was discussed up to the point of termination.

• Make a few written notes on the salient points of the discussion during the oral summary.

• Keep these notes in a conspicuous place for use at the time of the subsequent follow-through.

Making an assumption that one can quickly dispose of the call taking precedence and get back on the line to the other person usually doesn't work. Managers find themselves playing musical hold-button—jumping back and forth from one party to the other—and causing both consternation and confusion.

One can devote valuable time and concentration best to one conversation at a time. That's why managers ought not to ask anyone to wait on hold. For if the person tires of waiting and hangs up, the manager must regroup and start all over again.

One of the most flagrant inhibitors of effective listening takes place when the phone takes precedence over a person-to-person discussion that is already in progress. When a call is accepted in the presence of anyone, managers ought to reassure the person they are with that they'll return to their discussion promptly. Interminable waits while the phone conversation drags on are not only embarrassing and discourteous, they impose burdens on the listening process for both parties. When the phone discussion finally ends, comments such as "I'm sorry, where were we?" usually are insufficient and put the onus on the other person to put things back in order. This is unfair. If the manager has to take a call, it is his/her obligation to apologize for the interruption and ask the visitor to be patient *or* give the visitor the option of returning at a more convenient time if that is more practicable.

Nonurgent calls should not reach the manager in circumstances where others are available to answer the phone. However, when the manager must answer the phone himself/herself, and the call is not urgent, the person on the phone should be informed that the manager will be in touch again. The face to face conversation may then continue with listening unimpaired.

Managers must also be wary of needlessly extending telephone conversations beyond reasonable business limits. Excessive or nonessential socializing, for instance, causes both parties to forget why the business call was made in the first place.

To reiterate: When listening is a priority, the manager will exercise proper controls to ensure that all communications with all levels of persons are effective.

CREATING A VISUAL ATMOSPHERE THROUGH VOICE, TONE, PITCH AND INFLECTION

How does the manager sound to others when speaking on the phone? Perhaps you've been surprised by the sound of your own voice on audio tape. You may believe there's a significant difference between what you hear and how you always think you sound. Phone projection is the same, of course. The instrument itself causes a certain distortion of the voice. Therefore, it is particularly important that managers come across as persuasive and professional. Tone, pitch, and inflection play a vital role in getting others to want to listen. A dull, monotonous speaking voice is a big turnoff to any listener. Proper voice modulation and enunciation—supported by language that fits into the listener's frame of reference—add to the manager's credibility.

It usually takes only a modicum of concentration for others to listen. But it does take a conscious effort. Feelings, particularly negative ones, come across dramatically in one's tone of voice. A pleasant tone is always conducive to listening. To improve your phone communications, you might practice a few simple telephone greetings and test your phone voice. It can't hurt and, more than likely, you'll find others are more responsive because you're easy to listen to.

GETTING RESULTS FROM CONFERENCE CALLS

In today's high-tech, high-speed communications business world, the telephone takes on greater significance since costly and time-consuming person-to-person contacts are discouraged, particularly where offices or plants are spread out across the country or globe. This has made the conference call one of the manager's key tools for reaching others in the organization. With several persons participating in the call, and a relatively short time to communicate ideas and information, the importance of proper call planning, execution, and follow-through are magnified. To help the listening process and also make certain that adequate results are achieved from the communication, managers who conduct conference calls would benefit from doing the following:

- With the cooperation of the call participants beforehand, plan an agenda based on the requirements of the communication.

- Circulate the agenda to each participant, including separate notes to each that may help expedite the call. For example, reminding persons that they are expected to provide certain required inputs.

- Setting up an agreed-upon specific time for initiating the call, as well as communicating the estimated length of the call to participants.

- Arranging to have a third party place the originating call so that all persons are available and ready at the same time.

- Arranging to have a staff member record the discussion or take notes during the course of the call.

- Keeping on target by directing the discussion throughout. This will encourage listening and guide the discussion toward the desired objective.

- Crystallize key points during the course of the call orally.

- Summarize the outcomes of the call and pinpoint what is to be done next, if anything.

- Distribute written summaries of agreed-upon outcomes of the discussion, then follow through in whatever manner is necessary to be certain required actions are taken.

With everyone informed about the purpose of the call in the first place, the call conducted in a professional manner that keeps things in focus, and all persons informed about the outcomes, the listening process will evolve in an orderly and natural way.

8

LISTENING AT MEETINGS, CONFERENCES, SEMINARS AND LECTURES

Chapter 8 goals:

Provide listening guidelines for managers who attend meetings, conferences, seminars, and lectures where they often cannot exercise the kinds of controls common to one-on-one communications.

Whether by choice or otherwise, managers find their schedules often include attendance at meetings, conferences, seminars, and lectures. The control factors so vital to managing communications are limited in these types of activities. Often missing is the give and take associated with one-on-one discussions in person or by phone. Frequently, the manager feels like part of a captive audience, bombarded with someone else's messages and information, with relatively few opportunities, if any at all, to engage in the kind of exchange that helps the manager listen effectively. In addition, it is harder to concentrate and get the full benefit of what someone is saying when one is forced to rivet attention on that person for a period of time. The manager, normally an activator, feels put upon in a situation where he or she

101

remains passive, unable to contribute and move things along at a suitable pace or level of understanding. Managers need to find new ways of getting the most from listening at these seemingly passive sessions.

REVIEWING THE BENEFITS OF PLANNED LISTENING

When the boss asks for an oral report on the progress or outcome of a specific project on which the manager is working, the manager does not walk into the boss's office cold and begin talking about what has been done. Instead, the manager normally follows a more professional approach: Relevant data is gathered, assembled, and organized; the presentation, even if it is informal, is outlined, preferably in written form, and an appointment is made to see the boss. If it's necessary to check with the boss in advance of the meeting to be certain that essential items are included in the presentation, the manager will take care to do this.

As a result of this kind of preparation, the manager's imparting of information is crisp and to the point at the meeting. As discussed earlier, when a manager schedules an appraisal interview with an employee, the objective for the meeting is established, all relevant data is accumulated and organized, and, among other things, types of probes are considered that will help the employee benefit from the discussion.

Both of the above examples of a manager's communications with employees in the firm are given to reinforce the need for managers to know what they expect to achieve through all types of communications. It should be no different when the manager attends meetings, seminars, conferences, and lectures. The purpose in attending should be known in advance—listening then becomes the vehicle for achieving the purpose.

The best way I know to illustrate the close alliance between listening effectiveness, motivation, and having planned objectives is to describe the function and outcomes of an exercise I've incorporated in my course on listening.

In this course, attendees view a video presentation featuring a lecturer who talks about salesmanship. Prior to looking at the video, half the attendees receive information in writing telling them they are to assume they are newly hired sales agents attending a lecture on salesmanship. The other half of the class is given the same information but they receive additional background data in writing. This group is informed that:

- The speaker is a prominent person in the field and an official of the company for which they work.

- The title of the lecture is "The Common Denominator of Success."

- They are high achievers, determined to be in the top rung of their group in their first year of production.

- They should expect that the speaker will give them some specific guidelines for being successful in their work.

- They plan to review with their immediate supervisor the things they get out of the lecture that they believe will help them in their jobs.

Neither group is aware of the difference in instructions at this point.

The feedback is very interesting. Invariably, the self-starter group not only responds more positively to what the lecturer imparts in the way of advice for becoming successful in sales, they demonstrate a better understanding of the main intent of the presentation. All this tends to substantiate that when persons are prepared—psychologically and in other ways—to benefit from such presentations they listen for and detect central ideas in a more proficient manner. They also work at dealing with distractions of any kind that could keep them from meeting their objectives.

The benefits to listeners gained from having prescribed objectives are enormous. When the speaker really has something to say, they hear it and want to do something about it. They're not overwhelmed by the content and avoid trying to hang on to every word that is spoken. Their purpose guides their listening and gets them the results they are looking for. It's one more way of proving that when managers know where the goalposts are they'll know where to run with the ball. Knowing where to run makes it easier for them to plan how to get there.

OTHER LISTENING AIDS

What are some of the other ways that managers can achieve their listening objectives at meetings, seminars, conferences, and lectures? Taking notes while listening was discussed earlier (in Chapter Five). Managers can also help themselves be better notetakers, as well as better listeners, by also:

- *Using personal shorthand techniques*, such as abbreviations, shortened versions of words, topic headings, shorthand itself where it is part of their repertoire, underscoring key words and ideas that they've written, and other methods.

- *Editing their own note-taking.* A review of one's notes enables the listener to underscore or extract major items. This is a must for managers who plan to convert their notes in summary fashion, whether it be for communication with senior management, peers, subordinates, or others. Writing down only the essential items, in the first place, makes this an easier task to complete.

- *Audiotaping the live presentation.* This can be done provided permission is obtained in advance from the speaker. *Some bad points and pitfalls*: It's easy to forget to listen and avoid the "chore" of taking down written information; even when the recording device is checked out for reliability beforehand, malfunctions do occur and little or no recording takes place; the tape could be lost or misplaced (so could written notes, of course); in playback, other obligations/interruptions may prevent one from listening straight through, resulting in loss of train of thought or location on the tape where listening was abandoned temporarily; other activities or events may take precedence and there's a time lapse before getting to the tape for playback. *Some advantages*: Should it be necessary to leave the premises and thereby miss hearing part of the talk, the recording has it all down for reference; it serves as a permanent reference of the total oral experience that can be referred to by other persons who were unable to be present; listening to the presentation a second or third time may provide new insights about the message that were missed at the live session.

When note-taking, managers and others cannot afford to forget that the fundamental process of listening is *selection* of relevant information and key ideas and *retention* of what is valuable for the listener.

How Speakers Help Listeners

Speakers who are effective presenters help the listening process because their presentations:

- Immediately arouse interest in their subject.

- Let you know why it's important to hear what they say.

- Give you specific examples that substantiate their viewpoints.

- Suggest what you should do to benefit from what they've said.

Besides helping listeners identify and understand their main ideas through the careful organization of their talks, speakers also use *voice patterns* for emphasis. Inflection helps identify the major topics of the presentation; tonal quality helps highlight key words, phrases, or thoughts; a pause or silence at the right moment dramatizes a significant point. Effective listeners become attuned to these clues to meaning and are prepared to take notes accordingly.

How Visuals Help Listeners

Visuals help listeners as well. In some cases, particularly at seminars and conferences, presentors distribute written materials in outline and/or summary form. Also, workbooks containing essential information may be given to attendees who may be asked or required to record notes and certain key points. These workbooks become a primary reference source for summary and review of the major ideas and exercises from the session.

Transparencies, flip charts, design boards, etc., are also part of the multimedia approach that draws a listener's attention to items of special interest; the use of audio tapes and video tapes helps to dramatize pertinent elements.

SUGGESTED GUIDELINES FOR MANAGERS

Here are some proposed guidelines for the manager who is an attendee at meetings, conferences, seminars, and lectures.

1. *Know what you want to get out of the meeting*
   Whatever advance preparation you do will help you be a better listener. This includes knowing the purpose of the meeting, the format, what you're expected to contribute, etc.

2. *Let the meeting time be productive time*
   It's too easy to say "I could be doing something else that would be more beneficial" and as a result let your mind wander off to other things. If you're committed to be there, be there totally.

3. *Get involved*
   Be prepared to ask questions and make comments as an active member of the group. You won't say anything if you have little or nothing to contribute, but be heard when it counts.

4. *Avoid negative predispositions*
   Assume all persons, speakers and attendees alike, who have something to say at the meeting are likely to say something worthwhile. This way you won't miss out on anything that might be useful.

5. *Take notes*
Get central ideas and main points down on paper. They're good references during the course of the meeting and after the meeting is concluded.

6. *Broaden your attention span*
Observe everything that goes on by keeping your eyes open; hear everything that's said by keeping your ears open. This will help prevent "listening fallout"—the loss of the train of thought due to overconcentrating on one element of the session.

7. *Control your emotions*
Should an issue or statement get your adrenaline pumping and throw you off balance, take control of yourself quickly so you won't behave in a way that is disruptive. Better to be convincing by stating your position in a manner that makes others feel supportive. There's a big difference between being argumentative and being persuasive. However, if you blow a fuse, you might lose your ability to listen. Others, equally aroused, may also fail to listen.

8. *Position yourself for listening*
Choose a seat (wherever possible) that enables you to hear and see what's going on. It's amazing sometimes how many persons are careless about where they sit or stand. A nearsighted person should not get lost in the back of the room.

9. *Be diplomatic/tactful*
When you disagree with something that's been said state your point of view in a manner that leads to agreement. Overt responses such as "Oh, that's wrong" or "That won't work" tend to antagonize rather than convince. Support your position with facts.

10. *Understand group dynamics*

Be respectful of the rights of other members of the group to participate in the same way you do. They share the same privileges and compromise when necessary to maintain group solidarity. This means following general rules of decorum, e.g., letting others speak their complete thoughts without interrupting.

By actively following these guidelines managers get more out of meetings. Their constructive behavior makes others want to listen to them; they benefit personally by getting more out of what happens at meetings.

PURPOSES AND QUALITIES OF ELECTRONIC MEETINGS

When the factors of distance and time prohibit face-to-face discussions, managers use the telephone as the traditional method for exchanging information and ideas, discussing issues and problems. Conference calls (discussed in Chapter Seven) have the advantage of enabling groups of persons to reach one another simultaneously, thus speeding up the communications process considerably.

With further technological advances, more and more companies have turned to electronic meetings as a useful means of completing tasks that require group interaction. Managers who participate in these types of meetings are reaching a greater number of people inside and outside their organizations in ways that are more productive than ever before. The two primary forms of electronic meetings are *video conferences* (also known as *teleconferences*) and *computer conferences*. An examination of each will reveal their advantages and limitations, as well as describe the demands made on the manager to use positive listening practices for best results.

Video Conferences and Teleconferences

Video conferences are group-to-group meetings linking participants in one city with those in another. In addition to reducing travel and expenses of meetings, it allows managers to be in more than one place at one time. Participants in each location have the visual advantage of communicating both orally and visually with one another. Seated in their respective rooms, they are seen on video monitors. Cameras pick up the action, focusing on the entire group or individual members who are speaking at given points.

In reality it's no different from face-to-face communication in any other form except that there are more people involved than there would be in a single meeting room. Eye contact and nonverbals, therefore, are just as important, except that the focus is more extensive—the manager watches what happens in his own facility as well as the other location. The social element (do persons attending from both places know one another?) must be addressed early in order to move forward productively to achieve the meeting's objectives. Otherwise, the meeting is organized in much the same way as any other would be. In fact, facilitators are much more likely to ensure that agendas, objectives, and procedural matters are attended to properly, since wasted motion or weak direction in this kind of medium is highly conspicuous and more costly.

Computer Conferences

At computer conferences, participants type their messages to other conferees on standard computer terminals, usually linked by telephone to a computer network. Without images and voices, it doesn't resemble a meeting very much. Everything is recorded and indexed for access to memory. By exchanging information and sending messages many persons (often up to fifty) can communicate with one another over extended periods of time about a given subject or on a particular project.

One of the distinct advantages is that the typed message being sent can be put into a form acceptable to the sender before transmission, whereas the spoken word at "live" meetings becomes a part of the record as delivered even though restatement can be made on the spot. Typing skills help, but are not that critical.

Listening, then, is not a factor since composing messages in writing and reading messages received are the means of communicating.

Both *video conferences* and *computer conferences* work best when information needs to be exchanged, instructions are being given, and ideas are explored. Complex interpersonal types of communications, such as negotiation, generally do not lend themselves to these types of media.

9

LISTENING AS
THE MEETING LEADER

Chapter 9 goals:

Demonstrate that managers perform effectively as meeting presentors or chairpersons when they: Structure and organize the meeting to achieve desired objectives;

Promote listening through their understanding of group dynamics.

THE MANAGER
AS MEETING LEADER

Our emphasis so far has been on how a manager listens for main ideas and gets the most out of being a participant at meetings. Since hardly a week goes by in the business life of a manager without involvement in several meetings, it's particularly important to focus on the manager's role as a meeting leader.

As the organizer and/or conductor of a meeting, the manager must be prepared to be both an active listener and a catalyst for making things happen. In fact, the demands on the manager's ability to listen well are even more crucial when responsible for the successful outcome of a meeting.

How effectively he listens under these circumstances is dependent mainly on two key factors:

- How well the meeting is planned and executed.

- How effectively the manager performs as a presentor or coordinator of activities.

Meeting Planning and Execution

Regardless of what the subject of a proposed meeting may be or who the manager may choose to be in attendance, the first and foremost question that must be answered is "Is this meeting necessary?" Just because it's Monday morning, and the calendar shows that each Monday there's a scheduled meeting held for the staff, may not be sufficient reason for having the meeting. In answering this question the manager needs to determine if there is another, more practical way to accomplish the meeting objective without taking employees away from their jobs. Even when the meeting may last only a half hour, if several persons attend, the time expended is equivalent to the time factor multiplied by the number of people. That's when the manager might decide that it is not cost effective to have a meeting and, instead, chooses some other means of communicating. Also, managers need to remind themselves that employees are inclined to listen only tentatively when they feel the meeting they're attending has little value and they'd rather not be there at all.

CRITERIA FOR
SUCCESSFUL MEETINGS

A successful meeting—one that is timely, informative, and results-oriented—generally meets the following criteria:

- It is held at a time of day when the persons attending are not required to be elsewhere (on or off the job).

- It is held when the manager, or other person conducting the meeting, really has something to say or needs the input of the attendees.

- The meeting leader announces the meeting subject, time of day the meeting will be held, amount of time allotted, and place well enough in advance so all invited persons are able to plan to attend.

- It has a written agenda that includes the meeting purpose/objective, topics, and other pertinent information that will help the leader stay on target and serve as a guide for the attendees.

- It has one primary objective that attendees can relate to. Mixing apples and bananas distorts the purpose and could be confusing.

- It has a format that lends itself to obtaining the best results. Meetings held to introduce a new product, a sales idea, a new system, or a new service may differ considerably from one in which a common problem facing the group needs to be resolved. Some for instances:

    1. Panel discussions may be practical where experts with differing viewpoints are needed to stimulate the thinking of attendees.

    2. Motivational-type meetings should emphasize success stories. Where certain attendees have been successful their input helps. Plan their participation with them in advance. It will encourage the contributors to be at their best and build credibility for the topic.

3. Select other methods that will help achieve the results sought, e.g., have role-play exercises where skills development is essential; exercises that simulate on-job experiences, e.g., the in-basket; special games, etc.

- The room accommodations and room layout aid the listening process and are comfortable for attendees. Can everyone see the demonstrations? Can the speakers and others be heard? Transparencies projected on a screen usually are easier to read than handwritten flip charts. Regardless of what kinds of visuals are selected, they must be large enough and clear enough to be seen by everyone. Prepare the visuals in advance, when practicable. Stopping to write lengthy information on a flip chart delays the meeting and allows attendees plenty of time to let their minds wonder.

- At the start of the meeting distribute the agenda and other relevant materials, identify the objective and anticipated outcomes, clarify the format (questions and answers, participatory, lecture, questions held till the end of the session, etc.)

- Where attendees are required to take some kind of action as a result of the meeting, discuss it *at the meeting* and seek agreement. By waiting to do this after the meeting is concluded, problems or resistance may be encountered that were not anticipated and may be difficult to resolve.

- Particularly at participatory-type meetings, use probes to get persons talking. For instance: "Jim, you were telling me about the way you handled the Applebee account. . . . Tell us what you did and what results you got."

- Prepare and distribute written summaries as soon as possible after the meeting is concluded. The most effective summaries identify the meeting's highlights and spell out the type of follow-through on the outcomes, e.g., what attendees will do next. Where appropriate, the leader appoints an official notetaker (this is often done on a rotational basis by attendees) or a secretary is present who can transcribe rapidly and efficiently.

THE MANAGER AS AN EFFECTIVE PRESENTER

The preceding analysis demonstrates how the manager's ability to structure and organize a meeting helps attain the meeting objective. Of equal importance is how effectively the manager gets and keeps the audience's attention when performing as the principal speaker or session leader. Participants feel they are a part of the action and listen more attentively when the manager:

- Involves the audience through eye contact.

- Uses body language to support and complement the spoken words.

- Uses voice and language to convey meaning and generate interest.

Eye contact already has been identified as a vital aspect of "visual" listening in one-on-one situations. In the case of meetings, attendees tend to listen more attentively when they believe the speaker is interested in them. Effective presenters, acutely aware of this element of communication, deliberately focus their attention on individual members of the audience. They often do this by looking straight at the person for short intervals. When the eyes meet in this way, the participant believes—and rightly so—that the speaker is delivering that portion of the message especially for him or her. This carries over, and even when the speaker focuses elsewhere, the person so addressed continues to want to hear what's said.

This is not the only way a speaker makes an ally of each and every person in the group; nevertheless, it works, and it is significant in promoting positive listening. One way to prove the point is to ask you to consider what happens to any member of an audience when the presentor continually focuses on the floor or some other inanimate object and hardly ever, if at all, looks at anyone directly. When this happens, personal communication is lost and disinterest often sets in.

When it comes to letting *body language* support and complement what is spoken, the major difference between what was discussed earlier regarding body language and one-on-one listening and what happens at meetings, conferences, and seminars is that in the latter case more people are influenced at one time through this method of communication. Speakers cannot afford to neglect the significance of their posture and bodily movements as a means of gaining and keeping the audience interested in the subject. A true story may help illustrate this point.

A manager with multi-years experience in his department was commissioned by senior management to make a presentation about his department's work to groups of employees in branch office locations. Strangely, after all those years with the firm, he'd never spoken before an audience. He was apprehensive, fearful that he'd be ineffective, and also somewhat indifferent toward the whole project. He resisted the commitment until, by ultimatum, he was forced to prepare his presentation. At the training director's suggestion, he was invited to rehearse his presentation on videotape and get feedback on his effectiveness. In the playback he was pleasantly surprised to find one interlude where he seemed to be in control of what he was doing. Here's what he did at this juncture of his talk: He removed his glasses, gripped the side of the lectern, and leaned his body forward when making a critical point about his topic. After making the point he put his glasses back on and continued to "read" from his notes. His post-analysis of why he broke away from his prepared notes, stopped talking like a robot, and gave some feeling to his words through the use of his body was quite simple: "I really believed what I said there. . . . I guess I couldn't help doing what I did."

It was a valuable lesson for this manager, and helped him begin to believe in his ability to be able to get through to his audience. More important, when he used this same approach at the "live" sessions he had the chance to observe how his audience literally sat up and paid attention. Later, with additional coaching, he began to use his body to convey meaning in other parts of his prepared talk.

Earlier discussions of the use of one's voice in promoting listening centered primarily on telephone techniques. Similar principles apply to conducting meetings—tone, pitch, and modulation—the pleasantness inherent in the quality of the voice, the authority imbued in the resonance of the voice that commands attention at appropriate times, helps make the presentation flow and creates the kind of variety and pace that sustains an audience's interest.

Presentors must also be careful about how they use *language* to convey meaning. It is easy to overuse certain words in a repetitive fashion, for instance. One manager who addressed a group of employees for about forty-five minutes used the word "okay" close to fifty times. "Now, this is how to handle changes in the customer's account—okay?"; "When you talk with the customer on the phone, don't try to do all the talking—okay?" When the heavy use of this word was brought to the manager's attention, he registered surprise. He was not aware that "okay" was punctuated throughout his talk nor that it was proving to be a distraction that he needed to control. The next time he did a similar presentation he reduced the number of "okays" to fewer than ten, but managed to substitute the word "all right" in several places. After some counseling/coaching, he realized it would be practical to avoid this kind of redundancy.

Managers must also be wary of using words that may trigger negative responses. Saying "you people," for instance, even just a few times, gives the impression that the speaker is behaving in a condescending manner.

Nonwords, such as "and-a" used as stop-gap hesitations before proceeding to a new thought, also get in the way of a speaker's effectiveness and lose the audience.

GUIDELINES FOR CHAIRING A MEETING

There are times when the manager functions as a chairperson. In such situations the manager is an arranger of experiences, one who organizes and coordinates the meeting's activities. Some typical meetings of this type are:

• A committee, perhaps one appointed by the manager, meets to discuss the outcomes of a project.

• A panel of experts, often with differing viewpoints, addresses a group on a given subject.

• Employees meet to discuss a common problem or issue

where input is expected from all those attending. Sometimes meetings of this type are billed as "brainstorming" sessions where freewheeling, uninhibited discussion of a subject from all angles becomes the prelude for seeking a solution.

- A conference, with invited speakers who address a broad spectrum of items, e.g., a management development program.

The manager's main task at meetings where he/she acts as a chairperson is to:

- Set the stage for the discussion or presentation. As a part of the introduction the manager clarifies his/her role and goes over the ground rules for group participation. The manager comments on what he/she will do or will not do and what is expected of the attendees. For example: "Our panel will address [the subject]. After each person has spoken in the allotted time, you may present your questions for their response. We'll allow [time] for questions at the end of the meeting."

- Comment on the direction the meeting is taking by identifying issues, clarifying viewpoints expressed by speakers/attendees, crystallizing points of agreement/ disagreement, and summarizing at appropriate times in order to keep focus on the major topic.

The manager's ability to listen is fully tested when he or she is the chairperson. In a practical sense the manager must be conscious of everything that happens (or doesn't happen) in order to keep the meeting moving in the right direction. In this respect he or she is the most alert and attentive person present.

Here are a few of the characteristic situations that require some kind of action on the part of the manager as chairperson:

• The group attempts to come to a decision or draw certain conclusions, but gets hung up on a side issue that seems to throw things off center.

• Someone who has the floor is having difficulty communicating with the group. It may be a moment when the person can't seem to find the right word to express a thought; it could be when the person has said something that has caused confusion or misunderstanding.

• One or more attendees has, unnecessarily, diverted the attention of the speaker or members of the group.

• An emotional situation develops, or one appears to be developing, that could be disruptive.

In each of these typical situations the manager steps in to get things back on track or lend some kind of assistance. At all times the manager maintains an objective posture, demonstrating through his or her behavior total support for the group and its individual members. In effect the manager's neutrality acts as a stabilizing influence.

Chairpersons also:

• Know when to remain silent on the sidelines and permit the meeting to progress on its own terms. When things are going well the manager does not need to interject a commentary or offer more information.

• When it is inappropriate to interject comments without being disruptive the manager should make mental or written notes. Later, at a more convenient time during the meeting, these relevant thoughts can be expressed.

- Encourage attendees to contribute ideas and information through the use of probes that stimulate constructive thinking. Redirecting questions to selected persons is one method of helping the meeting move in the right direction.

- Compliment persons for particularly meaningful contributions. This may also be done subtly through nonverbal reactions that show approval.

- Use discretion in revealing subjective reactions or feelings. Don't permit posture, facial expressions, or demeanor to have a compromising effect on the group.

UNDERSTANDING GROUP DYNAMICS

It is always important for a meeting chairperson or speaker to understand what is customarily referred to as "group dynamics," i.e., the ways that groups respond to one another and the meeting's stimuli. This includes the group's responses to:

- The speaker—what is said and how it is said.

- The environment—facility and surroundings, such as lighting, ventilation, noise, etc.

- The topic under discussion and its implications for them.

- Individual members of the group—their physical presence in the room and their contributions, or lack of contribution, to the session. For instance, the way groups react to the attempt by one or more persons to take charge of the proceedings.

The orderliness of a meeting's progression does not depend entirely on the speaker's or chairperson's ability to maintain order or control. The group itself often shows it has the desire to supervise its own behavior. For example, individual members of a group usually respect one another's right to be heard but also clamp down when someone behaves in a way that they believe is detrimental to the best interests of the group. In most cases much depends on the purpose or mission of the group. If there is coherency to begin with, and it is fueled by high interest in what is taking place at the meeting, the group's behavior will be highly supportive. Unwittingly, perhaps, the cohesive group supports listening. The meeting presenter or chairperson who is highly attuned to the group dynamics process is better able to assist the group in its attempts to guide itself through the meeting's stages.

Final Perspective on Meetings

When a manager runs a meeting he must put to practical use all the avenues open for encouraging attendees to listen, participate, and take action. Besides considering what must be accomplished at the meeting, the manager should give consideration to what ought to be avoided: boredom, resentment, time-wasting. By controlling listening through well-run meetings, the manager gets the kind of feedback that promotes understanding and teamwork, and gets the job done in the most professional manner.

MAKING LISTENING PAY OFF
ON THE JOB

Chapter 10 goals:

Provide managers with guidelines for developing an action plan for making positive listening pay off on the job.

IDENTIFYING YOUR CLIENTS

The perceptive manager looks upon the great majority of persons inside and outside the organization as clients. Prospects, customers, subordinates, peers, bosses, and vendors alike all receive similar, attentive treatment. Prospects will, it is hoped, become customers; customers remain satisfied and provide additional business; subordinates make individual, outstanding contributions to the effectiveness of the operation and, as a group, are a powerful resource for achievement; peers may be great sounding boards for helping to solve problems and sound out new ideas; bosses can and will offer rewards for exceptional performance; vendors may give better or preferred service.

The perceptive manager also knows that listening contributes to the enhancement of his relationship with these clients; therefore, he develops and practices listening habits that bring him the kinds of results needed to be successful in his job.

Looking Backward and Looking Ahead

In previous chapters just about every aspect of listening that affects a manager's performance has been examined and, through case studies at the end of the book, you'll have practice in dealing with some of the more subtle and sometimes complex management situations in which listening is a factor.

At this point it would be easy and perhaps somewhat academic to go back chapter by chapter and identify the major subjects once more, hoping that this would reinforce your interest in being an effective listener. It is probably safer and more practical to assume that you've been making personal assessments about the way you listen on the job right along. More than likely you've already determined where you have decided strengths and where you need to improve. Therefore, the next logical step is to suggest that you'll be the beneficiary of your own guidance when you develop a *positive listening action plan*.

Here are some guidelines that may help make this a productive task.

ESTABLISH YOUR CRITERIA FOR LISTENING PERFORMANCE

Start by answering the question "Why should I be a Positive Listener?" In responding to this question, first give some thought to the broad picture. Consider:

• What you want to accomplish in your career.

- What your objectives are for managing your department.

- What it is about your style of managing that gets results.

As you reflect upon your own outlook and situation, keep in mind that managers who are most successful at listening have profiles that suggest the following characteristics:

- A positive image of themselves which they project to others.

- An organized plan for achieving their business goals. However, their outlook toward attainment of these goals is flexible. For instance, as they grow in their jobs and/ or find new paths that offer greater rewards or opportunities, they're able to change direction.

- A systematic approach to operating their departments. Their own rigorous performance requirements include: pinpointing work priorities; expeditious management of time; regular analysis of the effectiveness of work systems; constant evaluation of results. In addition, they diligently relate their contributions to the overall company effort.

- A realistic orientation concerning how to deal with people. Because their expectations of themselves and others are high, subordinates are apt to strive to live up to the confidence shown in them. Their leadership qualities usually are outstanding; their supervisory methods adaptive to the changing needs of the work group and the organization.

Next, think of the special features of *positive listening* and the benefits you and others derive. Some things to consider including are:

Features	*Benefits*
Positive listening creates a climate of trust where employees and others express their feelings freely.	It is easier to deal with problems and issues when everything is out in the open and the fear about speaking one's mind is dissipated.
Positive listening encourages employees and others to solve problems on their own.	Increased self-reliance leads to the acceptance of challenges and stimulates creativity. With subordinates, for instance, there's a stronger feeling of proprietorship about their jobs.
Positive listening fosters a partnership relationship between the manager and the client.	When interests and values are understood and shared, cooperation and mutual respect are keynotes of the work effort.

Compile your own list of *features* and *benefits*. It will help reinforce your perspective about why listening is one of the manager's most important and reliable communications tools.

After contemplating the broad picture, move on to the more specific. Reexamine your job responsibilities—those that you included in your "Job Inventory Checklist" from Chapter One. You may find it worthwhile to verify the accuracy of your original ratings concerning the relevance of the listening factor in each job category. You may even wish to change or add responsibilities as required. Where listening is critically relevant to carrying out any of the job functions/activities be certain you've carefully thought through how effectively you are using *positive listening* to get results.

This requires an objective analysis of your listening performance, a coming to grips as it were with whether or not your listening skills and habits are being used effectively to keep communication lines open with everyone. It means determining if you've converted the "no's" to "yes's" when you answered the ten questions about your listening attitudes in Chapter Two. If your objective response to any of those questions remains a "no," look again at the barriers that may be inhibiting your performance. Take another stab at getting at the root problem. Remember, it takes practice, as well as concentration, before some of the really tough barriers are overcome.

Sometimes the barriers are not that easy to uncover, let alone overcome. For instance, managers may not be ready or willing to admit that when they attempt to satisfy their ego needs they often fail to listen. Ego tends to make a manager talk instead of listen. When ego gets in the way, it's as if a manager is saying "See how smart I am. . . . I know all about what I'm saying, so let me tell you about it, then it will be self-evident as to why you should do what I'm recommending."

To compound matters the ego need gets strong support from the theory that managers inherently are take-charge types whose authority alone gives them credibility. It's as if they have a birthright to be persuasive. No wonder some managers automatically believe and behave as if they've got the solutions to everyone's problems at their fingertips.

Besides, managers are busy people with a big job to do. Since listening frequently requires wading through lots of extraneous information to determine the real message, there's often a tendency to step in and do the talking, and the thinking, for the other person. When this happens some people will give up and stop listening entirely. What's frightening is that one or two bad experiences make them inclined not to listen the next time the manager speaks with them.

Managers who have an awareness of how the ego factor may deter listening develop realistic controls to offset such tendencies. Among these controls are:

- Avoid prejudgments of people and information.

- Hear someone out fully before evaluating the message.

- Give full attention to the person with whom they're speaking.

- Resist the temptation to monopolize the conversation.

- Concentrate on the main points of the speaker's message when their minds begin to drift off to something else.

- Appreciate that not everyone may share or accept their beliefs.

- When there's disagreement, convince others with sound and reasonable arguments rather than cajole or become defensive.

As part of your objective analysis of your listening performance take another close look at the way you put probes to work in your communications. As you recall, probes help both you and the person with whom you are speaking keep the focus on the main intent of the communication. During face-to-face or telephone discussions with others remember why probes are useful aids to listening. They:

- Enable you to control the quantity and quality of information flow.

- Give you a direct line on another's knowledge, thinking, and feelings.

- Promote concentration on the subject under discussion by keeping things on course.

- Encourage two-way involvement, which in turn

  - Stimulates the natural flow of ideas/information

  - Helps surface prevalent attitudes and needs that may require your attention

  - Creates greater receptivity through understanding and empathy

- Reduce tension and build credibility through feedback.

Now review each and every way that you communicate with your clients—everybody in business with whom you have any kind of communication. Consider each aspect of your oral communications whether face to face or by telephone. Include:

Why you're communicating	What you are trying to accomplish; the way you structure and prepare your objectives.
What you say	The way you organize information and ideas so that the content of your message is understandable and acceptable.
Who you say it to	Consider your audience's point of view, experience, needs, interests, attitudes.

How you say it	Choice of words; selection of probes; voice patterns; the ways you support your words through eye contact, use of visuals, projection of unspoken messages.
What you hear and see	Interpretation and handling of verbal and nonverbal feedback.
Where you say it	The choice of location most appropriate to the nature of the communication (where choices are possible); how you use the physical setting to support your objectives.
When you say it	The timing of your message so that your audience is receptive.

POSITIVE LISTENING— PRACTICAL BUSINESS APPLICATIONS

Successful managers regularly practice *positive listening* in face-to-face discussions and telephone communications. Where planned meetings take place with clients (everyone managers are involved with in business), whether one-on-one or in groups, managers think ahead of time how to put *positive listening* skills to work. This includes telephone calls in which managers initiate the contact or, as in the case of conference calls, where the manager may be a participant but know in advance about the subject.

EXHIBIT 10A

Putting Listening Skills Into Practice
in Face-to-Face Communications

Positive Listening Preplan

- Have a clear understanding of the purpose of the discussion.
  —Identify outcomes sought by defining objectives.

- Have adequate knowledge of the main subject of the discussion.
  —Do additional research if information/ideas are lacking.

- Choose place and time that provide for open, uninterrupted communication and limited distractions.

- Consider the kinds of probes that may be useful in guiding the discussion.
  —Write down specific probes that could be asked.

- Be prepared to avoid distractions, resist biases, and keep emotions under control.

- Know which ways or means to measure the outcomes of the discussion.
  —Determine the kind and method of feedback that confirms objectives were met.

Positive Listening Discussion Plan

- Be conscious of the needs and interests of the other person; allow for differences of opinion.

- Give the other person opportunities to express complete thoughts.

- Concentrate on ideas and information rather than personalities.

- Use vocabulary that fits the situation and the persons frame of reference.

- Keep the voice patterns interesting through tonal variety and tempo changes.

- Use nonverbals that complement and reinforce what is said.

- Use eye contact to observe unspoken communications and demonstrate concern for the other person.

- Use probes that help keep the focus on relevant issues, needs, and information; provide feedback that confirms understanding.

- Achieve conviction through the choice of relevant examples/illustrations that support and clarify points of view.

- Resolve conflict or misunderstandings by seeking agreement; don't stifle conflict that takes a constructive course.

- Show honest reactions. For instance, be willing to admit judgmental miscalculations or allow that more time may be required to consider what was said or seek additional facts/information.

In every case—whether the communication is planned or unplanned, and no matter who it is that the manager is speaking with—*positive listening* strengthens interpersonal relationships. Exhibit 10A shows a typical *positive listening* approach for face-to-face communications.

Putting Listening Skills into Practice in Telephone Communications

There are only slight variations on the above *preplan* and the *discussion plan* in telephone communications. In the *preplan* stage all six items apply to telephone discussions, but managers might also clarify distractions to avoid:

- Accepting additional calls at the same time.

- Interrupting the call to attend to something else, thereby forcing one to keep the caller on hold.

Re the *discussion plan*: Since eye contact cannot occur and actual observance of nonverbal behavior (the manager's and the other person's) is not possible—except in the rare cases of a picture phone—managers must rely more heavily on letting their speech (language and voice qualities) convey meaning. Also, their consciousness level rises with regard to sudden changes in the other person's speech. A long pause at a point where the manager anticipates a verbal response may precipitate a probe by the manager to determine if the person is still following and accepting the train of thought.

DEVELOPING A POSITIVE LISTENING ACTION PLAN

We know that managers are spending upwards of 50 percent of their time every business day listening. That's a guaranteed 50 percent of the time that managers can help themselves and others meet their needs and accomplish tasks and assignments. When a manager puts *positive listening* into practice 100 percent of the time there has to be tremendous potential for getting results from all his communications.

One of the best ways to assure yourself that you have control of listening on the job is to develop a *positive-listening action plan*. This plan, in whatever form you organize it, doesn't guarantee that you'll be an effective listener. However, it can and will pinpoint what needs to be done. Evaluation of your needs and assessment of the advantages are the ingredients that make the plan workable.

The proposed *action plan* format that follows may help you develop your plan. The true measurement of the success of the plan depends on your perseverance in carrying it out and the benefits you see yourself and others attaining from putting it into practice.

POSITIVE LISTENING— GETTING THERE AND BEYOND

A *positive-listening action plan* that's put into practice, then reviewed and updated from time to time, can help managers strengthen their job performance. The plan becomes the manager's tool for identifying listening strengths and also spotting deficiencies that need correcting. It can work provided managers are prepared to admit certain things about themselves, the people with whom they work, and their organizations.

Some of the realities they must face are:

- *Change is often a slow, painful process.*

  The first step is to admit that improvement may be needed, then make a conscious effort to make it happen. Dispense with the fairy-tale outlook—it is rare indeed that movie stars are discovered seated at drugstore counters waiting to become overnight successes. The same holds true for managers—they become successful listeners by forming and practicing habits that make others responsive to them. All of that takes time and effort. Chances are if a manager determines he's got listening deficiencies others are also aware of them. Correcting or improving them, when it occurs suddenly, may confuse others at first because, good or bad, they're used to the old way. Legitimacy is established when you do something often enough to prove it's part of your

Positive-Listening Action Plan

━━

Measuring Listening Effectiveness

1. When I listen at meetings (as attendee/leader), listen in face-to-face discussions, and listen on the phone, how well do I:

	RATING		
	(High)		**(Low)**
	3	**2**	**1**
Project high expectations of myself and others			
Set realistic, attainable objectives			
Detect central ideas			
Overcome distractions.........			
Resist biases...................			
Defuse emotions...............			
Use eye contact			
Watch for nonverbal cues			
Perceive hidden messages			
Use nonverbals to support words			
Keep an open mind for ideas/ information			
Use clear language that's relevant to discussion			
Encourage two-way involvement...................			
Probe to clarify understanding and seek agreement...........			

Positive-Listening Action Plan _____
Use my voice to lend conviction
to my words.................... _____

Maintain a positive attitude
toward person speaking....... _____

Keep the focus on main
subject .... _____

Add any other skills/habits that are considered aids to
listening and rate them accordingly. For instance, a sales
manager might include, among other things, how well he/
she probes for a prospect's/client's initial needs; uncovers
objections and resistance.

	RATING		
	(High)		**(Low)**
	3	**2**	**1**
_____	_____		
_____	_____		
_____	_____		
_____	_____		
_____	_____		
_____	_____		
_____	_____		
_____	_____		
_____	_____		
_____	_____		
_____	_____		
_____	_____		
_____	_____		

2. Should any of these items be rated below my objective standards: What will I do to seek improvement? How will I know I've succeeded?

Listening Criteria	Ways to Improve	How to Measure Success
(Example)		
Use clear language that's relevant to discussion.	Use vocabulary that's closer to the understanding of my audience.	I know I've succeeded when I'm not stopping to explain the meaning of words and when my conversations move ahead more rapidly.
_____	_____	_____
_____	_____	_____
_____	_____	_____
_____	_____	_____
_____	_____	_____
_____	_____	_____
_____	_____	_____
_____	_____	_____
_____	_____	_____
_____	_____	_____
_____	_____	_____
_____	_____	_____
_____	_____	_____
_____	_____	_____

3. What are the real benefits from positive listening for myself/others/organization?

(Examples)

Shorter, more effectively run meetings

Fewer unresolved problems

More highly motivated employees

_____

_____

_____

_____

_____

_____

_____

_____

_____

_____

_____

_____

_____

_____

_____

_____

_____

_____

_____

makeup. Work at it, and others will come around to accepting it.

• *It's best to concentrate on essentials.*

It may be nice to have an automobile with a plush interior, air conditioning, a stereo, a telephone, and anything else that's considered an "extra," but without the four wheels and other required parts the car isn't going anywhere. The analogy can be applied to a manager's total performance. Perhaps the "four wheels" for the all-around, competent manager are:

1. *Technical superiority* in the manager's field/profession.

2. *Analytical talents* that enable the manager to identify and solve complex work problems.

3. *Social skills* that make the manager pleasant to deal with and persuasive.

4. *Positive listening skills* that strengthen interpersonal relationships and keep the focus on meeting performance objectives.

Weakness in one or another detract from the manager's overall effectiveness. Yet, because managers interact in all aspects of their work, the listening factor takes on added significance.

• *Managers may not give proper credit to their listening ability.*

Think of some recent experiences where you were pleased with the outcomes of what may have been a pretty tough communication for you to handle with someone. What did you do that worked in resolving a problem or getting the action you wanted? There's a pretty good chance that your ability to practice *positive listening* played a part in the resolution. Think about that, and see if it's true.

- *Managers can't use* positive listening *today and turn it off tomorrow.*

    Listening well is a lifelong process. Managers can't be good at it with the boss but not so good at it with those in their client group. And they can't be good at listening with the boss one day, then not so good the next day. The consciousness level must always be high. A good habit that is formed must be used again and again until it is a regular part of the manager's behavior pattern.

- *Not everyone hears something the same way.*

    That magnificent lady Gracie Allen once said about her partner and husband, George Burns, "George didn't listen to what I heard." She made the statement in reply to someone's telling her, "Gracie, you didn't hear what George told you."

    Gracie's comment may seem weird, but if you read between the lines, there's more there. Sometimes we think we've expressed our ideas in a straightforward or eloquent manner, only to find out that not everyone has heard what we said the same way. We've got to reshape the same message for different people in order to have it understood, and sometimes we have to say it several times in various ways to get our ideas across. Interestingly, others may have the same problem communicating with us.

- *Where does the motivation to listen come from?*

    In the final analysis, the manager is the key to his or her own listening success. Your inclination to control or guide your communications with others takes shape when there's a definite purpose in mind, a goal in sight, a substantial need to be met.

Look at the way we're motivated to behave with doctors. When we don't feel well, we seek out a physician to diagnose our symptoms or relieve the pain. At the conclusion of the visit, when we're given a prescription or told what to do or what not to do to help ourselves, we listen very carefully. This is a personal thing that we take seriously. The fact that we're laying out good dollars to get expert advice creates an incentive to follow what we're told to do. The critical factor, however, is our concern about our health. Since we value our health and want to protect it, we listen and we retain information.

In a comparable way, listening becomes an incentive in business when we get serious about it—and we're usually serious when we care enough to make it a priority in our daily work. You've been examining the reasons why *positive listening* is essential to your success. How strongly you see the need to make it work for you will likely be the motivating force that helps you become and remain a *positive listener*.

APPENDIX

In this appendix you'll find a variety of case studies in which typical situations involving listening skills are presented. Following this case is my commentary of how the situation should be handled.

TESTING YOUR
LISTENING EFFECTIVENESS
—CASE STUDY ANALYSES

Appendix goals:

Provide practice in dealing with a variety of listening situations/problems that managers often face in business. Should you find yourself involved in similar situations or have to deal with like problems, your current analysis of the case studies ought to be of benefit.

Our emphasis has been on the manager as a controller of the listening process. This means managers not only know *how to* listen, they also know *why* they are listening. You've also seen that by generating meaningful dialogues and directing discussions toward a desired result where all participants benefit, managers maintain command of their communications. Probes were identified as one of the primary methods used to achieve these ends.

145

HOW CASE STUDIES
HELP MANAGERS DEVELOP
POSITIVE-LISTENING SKILLS

Case studies developed from actual incidents in business and those based on hypothetical circumstances provide managers with opportunities to test their ability to use their listening skills effectively. Keep in mind as you read and study each case that the major concern is how the manager controls the total communications process. Listening, then, is a means to an end.

Some of the cases direct attention to specific problems that managers face when they listen to others or try to get others to listen to them. Other cases offer much more subtle variations on the theme of listening. These require a broader, if not deeper, analysis.

For example, when someone creates a highly tense atmosphere by speaking or acting in an emotional manner, they may create resentment or resistance on the part of the person with whom they're communicating. As a result the other person "hears" negatives and so responds most often in a negative or defensive way. However, if managers determine in all their oral communications that they wish to create an atmosphere in which a person wants to listen to them, tends to hear what they really mean, and then does something appropriate about it, they'll avoid contributing to the kinds of circumstances where the listening effort is impaired or thwarted, such as appearing threatening or intimidating.

In truth, even with the best of intentions, managers are not always satisfied with their behavior and find themselves thinking "I shouldn't have done it that way" or "I shouldn't have said that; look how things got fouled up." Yet, when managers are in control of the listening process, such occurrences are less frequent. When they do happen, however, managers seek ways to rectify the situation. If it's too late to take immediate steps to alter the effect of what has taken place, managers seek ways to alleviate the situation and make certain the same "mistake" is not made again.

The case studies presented on the succeeding pages will be of greatest benefit when these procedures are followed:

- Read the case in its entirety, including the questions at the end.

- Jot down your responses to the questions in the spaces provided.

- Read the author's analysis of the case, then compare it with your analysis.

- Reflect on both interpretations (yours and the author's) and select those elements that you find most useful.

- Where appropriate, mark your original response to reflect any additions, deletions, or changes in your thinking.

When you examine how you'd behave, then scrutinize a "second opinion," you ought to come away with a greater appreciation of how to be a positive listener, as well as understand how you can guide others to be positive listeners.

CASE STUDY ANALYSIS

The Restaurant Manager
(Customer Relations)

You are the manager of a restaurant and act as the maître d'. You enjoy the business and take pride in having a clientele that visits your establishment time and time again.

You frequently get compliments about the food, the ambiance, and the excellent service.

Recently you hired a college student named Scott Harrington as a waiter. As is your practice, you trained him personally, reviewing all requirements for doing his job. In particular you stressed the importance of maintaining a pleasant disposition and tone with customers. You also told him that it was a practice for waiters and waitresses to give their names when addressing customers.

Last evening one particular couple entered the restaurant for the first time. You seated them at one of Scott's tables. During their stay you casually observed Scott and were impressed with his manner and efficiency. In particular you remembered his greeting to the couple: "Good evening, my name is Scott, I'll be your waiter. May I get you something from the bar?" You complimented him when he completed his shift.

The next evening the same couple returned and you expressed your pleasure in seeing them again so soon. Although you took them to a different area of the restaurant from the previous night, Scott was their waiter since he was working a new station. You signaled Scott to let him know you'd just seated the customers. Scott started in their direction. As you were leaving the area you overheard the following:

Woman Customer (to escort): Darling, I loved the prime rib last night, but tonight I want to try something a little different—perhaps some seafood. Oh, look we've got the same waiter. Hello, Scott! How are you?

Scott: Good evening! My name is Scott. I'll be your waiter. May I get you something from the bar?

What is Scott's listening problem?

_____

_____

_____

_____

_____

How should the manager approach Scott about the situation?

_____

_____

_____

_____

What should the manager do to help Scott improve his listening skills?

_____

_____

_____

_____

_____

What should the manager do to avoid similar problems with other waiter trainees?

_____

_____

_____

_____

_____

CASE STUDY
ANALYSIS SUMMARY

The Restaurant Manager
(Customer Relations)

What is Scott's listening problem?

Scott is concentrating so hard on "giving" information that he has been overprogrammed. He's not listening with his ears, and he's not listening with his eyes. He might have remembered the couple from the previous night had he also programmed himself to remember faces as well as lines. In his defense it is possible to forget having seen some people, but there are very few good reasons for not hearing someone who addresses one directly.

How should the manager approach Scott about the situation?

Truthfully say that he overheard the conversation, paraphrasing what was said, and ask Scott for his reaction.* This will help the manager learn if Scott really understands that he goofed. Chances are Scott will indicate he had not heard what the lady said (for whatever reason) or he would have responded differently.

What should the manager do to help Scott improve his listening skills?

Coach him. Suggest that since he has the greeting under control, he should focus on each customer by paying them immediate attention. While attending to his customers he

---

* It's important to ask for Scott's input before giving advice or information. Better for Scott to correct his own mistakes/shortcomings. As a result, he'll be a better listener when the manager has constructive criticism.

should be more conscious of the way they look (physical features, clothing, etc.) and tune them in when they speak to him. Make sure Scott understands the advantages of improving his listening skills—higher tips, perhaps; customers asking for him when they return to the restaurant; good business for the restaurant; job security.

What should the manager do to avoid similar problems with other waiter trainees?

Include in his orientation program information about the advantages of listening to customers. This would include being alert to what they say and retaining information about them. In other words, reinforce his feelings about the standards for dealing with customers and what he believes will help the waiter/waitress be more effective.

CASE STUDY ANALYSIS

The Stockbroker and the Marketing Executive (Telephone Communications)

You are a young stockbroker, Jane Hace, in a brokerage firm. You've done extremely well in the first eight months since you've been registered to deal with the public. You pride yourself in your ability to help your clients meet their investment objectives. You are especially careful to give each person individual treatment.

Recently you began a new prospecting program designed to add to your client base. You've been particularly successful. It seems investors are attracted to you because you give them personalized service. This type of service includes reviewing their needs and objectives and recommending stock and bond trades that fit their portfolios.

Yesterday several of your newer clients phoned and inquired about why you had not recommended a certain pharmaceutical stock. They'd seen an ad in the local newspaper where your firm recommended the stock as a good buy at its current price. It was the first time an ad like this had appeared and you were unprepared to deal with it. You're upset now because you were uncertain about what to tell your clients. Your manager is out of town on business, so you placed a call to the marketing director, Rick Johnson. This was the conversation:

RICK: (answering phone) Rick Johnson, Marketing.

JANE: Hello! This is Jane Hace from the Cincinnati office.

RICK: Good morning, Jane. What can I do for you?

JANE: Listen, Rick, I'm a little upset about something....

RICK: I'm sorry.... What can I do to help?

JANE: I don't understand... what's the idea of putting an ad in our local paper telling clients they ought to invest in Triple Ex Pharmaceuticals.

RICK: Oh! What's wrong with that?

JANE: There's plenty wrong. I plan my clients portfolios very carefully, and right now I don't find Triple Ex the best buy in the market. So what do you think happened? I've gotten a rash of calls from investors asking me why I didn't recommend Triple Ex when my company is pushing it in the papers. Now they think I'm misleading them.

RICK: Jane... when your clients called, what *did* you sell them?   (LONG PAUSE)

JANE: Excuse me. I've got to take care of something right away. I'll call you back.

If you were Jane Hace, what would you say to the marketing director when you returned the call with a response to his final question?

_____

_____

_____

_____

If you were Rick Johnson and did not hear from Jane Hace within a reasonable period of time (perhaps two days), would you call her back? If "yes," what would you say?

_____

_____

_____

_____

If you were Jane Hace and had placed the original call to the marketing director, would you have approached him any differently?

_____

_____

_____

_____

What limitations or problems resulted from dealing with this subject via a telephone call?

_____

_____

_____

_____

CASE STUDY
ANALYSIS SUMMARY

The Stockbroker
and the Marketing Executive
(Telephone Communications)

If you were Jane Hace, what would you say to the marketing director when you returned the call with a response to his final question?

I'd indicate that I'd misunderstood the intention of the ad and apologize for not having thought it through more carefully before calling. I'd also thank Rick for asking me the question "What did I sell them?" I'd admit that I had missed a golden opportunity to try for additional business and that I'd be ready to do it right the next time. I'd probably also inquire as to when the next ad might be appearing, so I could anticipate these types of calls.

If you were Rick Johnson and did not hear from Jane Hace within a reasonable period of time (perhaps two days), would you call her back? If "yes," what would you say?

Yes, I would call her back. As marketing director, I'm concerned that all salespersons know how the firm supports their efforts. The ad in the paper was one such instance. I'd say something like "I didn't mean to put you on the spot the other day when we spoke about Triple Ex Pharmaceuticals. I should have clarified why we place ads in local papers all over the country." I'd pause here in anticipation that Jane may have already figured it out and would provide an explanation similar to that described in response to the question above. If Jane did not do this, I'd explain how the ads are designed to stimulate prospect and client contacts.

Since Jane is a conscientious broker and an astute planner for her clients, she'd likely indicate she knows how to take advantage of such contacts. Through additional probing, if necessary, I'd help her see that the marketing department wants to support her efforts.

If you were Jane Hace and had placed the original call to the marketing director, would you have approached him any differently?

Yes, I would have explained that my manager was out of town and I thought Rick could explain the purpose of the ad, without revealing that it had caused me consternation.

Jane may not have the title "manager" (probably no one reports to her directly); nevertheless, she's an entrepreneur who manages her clients investments. Therefore, she must be able to think and behave as a manager. She should exercise good judgment and say to herself, in effect, "There must be a purpose to the placement of that ad that eludes me, so I'd better ask 'why,' even if the explanation may turn out to be quite simple—one that I should have figured out for myself."

An intelligent probe addressed to the marketing director, saying something like "Rick, regarding the ad for Triple Ex Pharmaceuticals, maybe you'd explain why we're pushing the stock?" would get her a straight answer. This makes her less vulnerable to facing the embarrassment caused by the original outburst, in which she may have created the impression that the marketing department doesn't know what it's doing by placing the ad.

Sometimes it is tough to figure things out in advance as carefully as has been suggested. It's easier to respond spontaneously, the way Jane did in the initial call, then handle things from there. But managers can't afford to do that. They need to listen first, then react. Jane's behavior showed she wasn't prepared to listen, she wanted to be critical instead. Yet, a single probe, such as the aforementioned, could have lead to a quick clarification and saved Jane some frustration and embarrassment.

Managers get back on the track when these things happen by attempting to be completely honest with themselves and the people with whom they are dealing.

What limitations or problems resulted from dealing with this subject via a telephone call?

Both the marketing director and the stockbroker did not have the advantage of interpreting nonverbal clues. Instead, there was total reliance on content of message and interpretations of voice qualities (tone, inflection, etc.). Managers need to be especially conscious of how they sound to compensate for the missing nonverbals. Also, it was too easy for the call to be terminated before some kind of resolution of the issue(s) could take place. Neither the marketing director nor the stockbroker could afford to "drop" things, but it was clearly the responsibility of the stockbroker to make the first move in dealing with the unresolved issues raised by the original call.

CASE STUDY ANALYSIS

The Product Manager
(Delegation—Time Expediency)

You are the product manager over a line of ready-made suits and sports coats for a men's clothing manufacturer that makes business and casual wear for several well-known labels. You have a small staff of employees who help you to seek new contracts, service existing customers, and package marketing approaches.

You are about to leave on a business trip to negotiate a contract with a textile supplier. However, you are concerned that you also have a number of phone messages that you should return but don't really have the time to do so. You decide to have David, your best employee, return the calls for you. You call him to your office and tell him that you must run out in two minutes, and would he please return the calls for you.

When you return the following Tuesday you are pleased that as well as handling his own work, David has returned all of your calls for you. Several of them he handled in close to the same manner that you would have. Three, though, were disasters. David just didn't know what you had been involved in and what you had agreed to with those customers. Consequently, two customers now think that your company doesn't know what it is doing, and one managed to convince David to meet an expedited delivery schedule despite the fact that the customer is grossly delinquent in paying for already delivered merchandise.

Other than saving you time, what were the positive aspects of your having David return your calls?

_____

_____

_____

_____

What was David's problem?

_____

_____

_____

_____

How could you have prevented the problem? (Be creative in your answer.)

_____

_____

_____

_____

_____

CASE STUDY
ANALYSIS SUMMARY

The Product Manager—
(Delegation—Time Expediency)

Other than saving you time, what were the positive aspects of your having David return your calls?

David showed initiative in taking care of these items for you. He also had the chance to speak with several customers and got some business matters taken care of.

What was David's problem?

David tried to handle too much. In the case of the "disasters," had he really listened to what the customers were communicating, he would have realized he needed your input before trying to resolve anything. Apparently he wished to exercise authority where the authority did not really exist.

How could you have prevented the problem? (Be creative in your answer.)

You might have done one or both of the following:

(1) Indicated to David that if anything seemed to be more than routine you'd want him to get the facts and discuss things with you before taking action.

(2) Taken five minutes or less to screen your messages before you left the office, then briefed David on those that might require special handling. Certainly he could have known in advance that he ought to be wary about making any commitments in the case of the delinquent paying customer.

CASE STUDY ANALYSIS

The Customer Service Department Manager (Coaching)

You are the manager of the New York customer service department for a company that provides information about computers that your company leases to its customers. Most of your customers are in a highly competitive industry and are under a great deal of pressure. Your customers tend to "spread" that pressure around whenever they think that your company is falling down on the job. One of the most important things for you and your employees to do is to keep your cool when speaking with often less than rational customers.

Barbara, one of your customer service reps, recently transferred into your department and has unusually fine knowledge about your company's services and operations. All she lacks is some self-confidence that you think will build over the next few weeks.

Just a few minutes ago you overheard Barbara speaking with what must have been an irate customer. One of the things you heard her say was, "What do you mean I'm not

listening to you! You're not listening to me!" It went somewhat downhill from there.

What was the probable outcome of the communication?

_____

_____

_____

_____

_____

What prevented the two parties from communicating?

_____

_____

_____

_____

_____

What can you do to help prevent future similar incidents?

_____

_____

_____

_____

CASE STUDY
ANALYSIS SUMMARY

The Customer Service
Department Manager (Coaching)

What was the probable outcome of the communication?

Frustration at both ends. The chances are nothing much was resolved because both parties were behaving in an accusatory manner with Barbara as the precipitator.

What prevented the two parties from communicating?

Each became emotional and tried to fix the blame for failure to communicate on the other person.

What can you do to help prevent future similar incidents?

Sound out Barbara on what she believes was the real problem in dealing with the customer. Concentrate on issues rather than personalities. See if you can both agree on what kinds of information will help the customer understand Barbara's position and also help Barbara comprehend what the customer may have been trying to convey to her.

Review and clarify alternatives for responding in an emotional way. Get Barbara to suggest these alternatives before offering your own. Barbara needs to know that by saying "What do you mean I'm not listening to you! You're not listening to me!" she can only antagonize and prevent others from dealing with the subject in a rational manner.

CASE STUDY ANALYSIS

The Production Control Manager (Customer Relations)

You are in charge of production for a medium-sized electronics subcontractor. It's not unusual for you to meet with customers to discuss production specifications, standards, and delivery schedules.

Today you are meeting with a representative of a major

aerospace company that is here to discuss details concerning electronic controls that will be produced in your shops to military specification standards.

You pride yourself on having an open-door policy which allows your employees access to you whenever they need your ear. Several times during your meeting with the aerospace company official you are interrupted by calls from the production line, all of which you accept and answer with obvious expertise.

When your visitor leaves he seems less happy than when he came in. First thing the next morning your boss calls you on the carpet to discuss why the aerospace company is considering taking their business to another subcontractor.

What went wrong, and why?

_____

_____

_____

What can you do to prevent similar problems in the future while still maintaining your open-door policy?

_____

_____

_____

_____

_____

_____

_____

_____

_____

CASE STUDY
ANALYSIS SUMMARY

The Production Control Manager
(Customer Relations)

What went wrong, and why?

Your visitor was disturbed because he did not get your undivided attention, to which he thought he was entitled. He was made to feel an inconsequential part of your daily routine. He probably interpreted this as your way of expressing disinterest in doing business with his company.

What can you do to prevent similar problems in the future while still maintaining your open-door policy?

Inform your secretary that you are not to be interrupted at the beginning of your discussion with your visitor. Saying this to her as the visitor enters your office will help make it clear that his best interests are also your best interests.

Have someone (your secretary or others on your staff) who has access to incoming calls screen the calls carefully and not interrupt except in emergencies.

When an interruption cannot be prevented, apologize to your visitor and ask his indulgence while you handle a pressing matter. Chances are he'll understand and be patient.

CASE STUDY ANALYSIS

Interviewing Job Applicants
(Developing Spontaneous Probes)

You've prepared for a job applicant interview by examining the application completed by the interviewee. You've also reviewed the qualifications for the job. You've determined which types of probes might be useful and made a list of those that you plan to use.

As an interview progresses, applicants will make statements from time to time that will require additional, spontaneous probes on your part. You seldom can anticipate what the applicant will tell you.

Here are some kinds of statements applicants may make, either in response to questions you ask or they may volunteer the information. Although these statements are out of context you will benefit from practicing the kinds of responses that seem most appropriate. Read the comment, and in the space provided enter how you might respond.

Applicant's Comment   *How You Might Respond*

No one seemed to
care about what I
thought about my
work.

I never thought I'd
get a promotion.

My supervisor
wasn't the easiest
person to get along
with.

About the position,
can you give me an
idea of what I'll be
required to do?
(Asked by applicant
soon after the start
of an interview.)

CASE STUDY ANALYSIS SUMMARY

Interviewing Job Applicants (Developing Spontaneous Probes)

Applicant's Comment	*How You Might Respond*
No one seemed to care about what I thought about my work.	Make a *neutral* comment, e.g., "That's very interesting...." (Then pause.) If applicant gives no further response use an *open* probe, e.g., "Can you explain what you mean?"
I never thought I'd get a promotion.	Remain silent and look directly at applicant. If no further response, use an *open* probe, e.g., "Oh, what made you think you'd never get a promotion?"
My supervisor wasn't the easiest person to get along with.	You could use an *open* probe, e.g., "Why do you say that?" You might get a more objective response and one that is more valuable to you by asking "What are the things you look for in a supervisor?"
About the position, can you give me an idea of what I'll be required to do?	From your standpoint, but perhaps not from the applicant's, this question is asked prematurely. You are not yet prepared to discuss elements of the job. You are more concerned with determining the applicant's qualifications. Indicate that it's a good question and that you'll be telling her/him all about the job shortly.

CASE STUDY ANALYSIS

The Disgruntled Employee
(Silence in Listening)

Subordinate: I had a bit of an argument with Joe in Accounting this morning about the report he owes us.

Manager: Oh!

Subordinate: You know, I've always thought he delayed getting the report done because he had it in for me for some reason.

Manager: Is that so?

Subordinate: Sometimes that guy gets me so angry.... He seems to think that just because he's worked on these kinds of projects so long, he knows all the answers. It's his indifference that really annoys me, though.

Manager: Uh, huh!

Subordinate: Every time I remind him that we need the report, he just glares at me, then goes back to doing something else, as if I'm not really there at all. He always claims he's got lots of people to take care of.

Manager: (Remains silent)

Subordinate: As far as I know I've never done anything to offend him. I wonder if he treats everyone the same way. But I am concerned about getting that report to you.

Manager: (Nods in agreement)

Subordinate: I don't know ... maybe I should try a different approach with Joe, like lay off him awhile and see what happens. Yeah, that's what I'll do. It could be he just doesn't like being bugged for something all the time.

What do you perceive to be the advantages to the manager in remaining silent through most of the dialogue?

_____

_____

_____

_____

_____

If you were the manager what would influence your decision to let the employee talk through the problem without inter-jecting your own thoughts/observations?

_____

_____

_____

_____

_____

If you were the manager would you add anything at the end to what was already said? If "yes," what would you say?

_____

_____

_____

_____

_____

_____

_____

_____

_____

CASE STUDY
ANALYSIS SUMMARY

The Disgruntled Employee
(Silence in Listening)

What do you perceive to be the advantages to the manager in remaining silent through most of the dialogue?

When employees are experiencing difficulties in dealing with a situation, they're often looking for a sounding board for working out minor irritations or frustrations. Under these circumstances there isn't much that a manager can say. By remaining silent or by showing that one is listening by means of neutral probes or nonverbal responses, employees can get something off their chests and, as they do, draw their own conclusions about what they should or shouldn't do.

If you were the manager what would influence your decision to let the employee talk through the problem without interjecting your own thoughts/ observations?

My experience in dealing with the employee in similar kinds of circumstances would be a factor. Whether or not it was critical to get the report quickly, would have to be considered. I'd also be sensitive to how my comments might influence the employee's point of view. As the person in authority it would be better to see if the employee has any solutions first.

If you were the manager would you add anything at the end to what was already said? If "yes," what would you say?

I'd probably second the subordinate's thought that a different approach in dealing with Joe was a good idea.

Again, depending upon the critical nature of getting the report in on time, it might be advisable to let the employee know how long I could wait. Also, I'd consider asking the employee if there was anything he or she needed me to do to help the situation, but only if I felt the employee was having some real problems handling the matter.

A supportive statement might be appropriate, such as "You may be correct . . . Joe probably does get a lot of pressure from other areas. It may be best to lay off for a few days. If that doesn't work, let me know if I can help."

CASE STUDY ANALYSIS

The Systems and Methods Project (Delegation—Subordinate Relationships)

On Monday of last week, Hank Swenson, the manager of the Systems and Methods section of a large financial services organization, asked three of his supervisors to determine how successfully a new data-processing system had been installed in selected departments in the firm. The assignments were as follows:

Accounting—Jack Marshall

Marketing—Sarah Ridgeway

Personnel—Larry Hemingway

Each person was instructed to take one week to compile data, then to meet the following Monday with Swenson to review their progress. They were also informed that they would be required to prepare a written report for upper management after the meeting.

All three persons were acquainted with the new system; in fact, they had a hand in formulating some of the policies and procedures recently adopted.

Each was told that the preliminary oral report should include the following:

- How well employees had accepted the change from the old way to the new way.

- What problems, or kinks, remained that should be ironed out.

- What, if any, new changes in procedure were needed to implement the total package successfully.

Jack and Sarah were experienced persons who had handled similar assignments in the past; however, this was Larry's first opportunity to follow through on this kind of project on his own. Here is what transpired at the Monday meeting between Hank and Larry:

HANK: Good morning, Larry, how are things going in Personnel?

LARRY: Well . . . as you know, this is my first time on this kind of project. I'm anxious to do it right. I want you to know that.

HANK: I'm glad you reminded me. In fact, this meeting will help you discuss what you found. If things are going well, that's fine. However, if there are problems, we need to know what they are so we can deal with them. So go slowly . . . and tell me how the new system is working.

LARRY: I'm not sure where to begin.   (Pause)

HANK: Take your time . . .   (Silence) Larry, how helpful were the written guidelines I gave you for checking out each item?

LARRY: I'm glad I had them. I might have been working in the dark without them.

HANK: Why don't you start with the first item on the list—"How well have the employees accepted the new system?"

LARRY: Well . . . Employment, Medical, Training, and . . . Employee Relations have things under control.

HANK: That's fine. Are they getting their reports in on time with complete information?

LARRY: Yes! All the supervisors, most of whom I'd never met before, were very cooperative.

HANK: I'm glad to hear that. But are *you* satisfied that the reports are up to the standards we set?

LARRY: Yes, I am.

HANK: Good! Now . . . you mentioned several sections. How about the others?

LARRY: Well, there's only one more. Compensation. And that's where there's some trouble.

HANK: What kind of trouble is that?

LARRY: Well, to put it bluntly, they like the old system better and they're not really getting the job done the new way.

HANK: What do you mean "not getting the job done the new way"?

LARRY: They're using the new system, but they're keeping their records on the old report.

HANK: When did you find this out?

LARRY: Compensation was the last section I checked, so that was Friday.

HANK: I see! What did you do about it?

LARRY: I sat down with the supervisor, Jerry Rank, and asked him to explain the problem. He told me he had trouble getting some of the senior clerks to write up the new reports. (Pause)

HANK:	Uh . . . huh! Go on . . .
LARRY:	Then he got a call and said he had to go to a meeting.
HANK:	You realize the new reports have to go to Data Processing by Wednesday?
LARRY:	Yes, I do.
HANK:	What did you say to Jerry?
LARRY:	I've got a meeting with him at eleven today.
HANK:	And what will you do?
LARRY:	I'm going to lay it on the line. He's got to scrap the old reports and use the new format.
HANK:	Do you think he'll buy that?
LARRY:	Yes, I'll see to that.
HANK:	Will he move fast enough to meet the deadline?
LARRY:	I'll see to that too.
HANK:	Will you need any help from our staff? (Sound of buzzer for intercom) Excuse me. (Speaks into box) Yes?
SECY:	I had to interrupt. The president wants to see you in fifteen minutes.
HANK:	Yes, tell him I'll be there (To Larry:) Let's see . . . you said you've got a meeting with Jerry today about getting the new reports done correctly . . . and you don't need any help.
LARRY:	Yes. I'll handle it. Even if I have to work with the clerks myself in getting the changes made, the report will be in on time.
HANK:	All right, Larry, I'll leave that up to you. But keep me posted on your progress. If you suspect any complications, I need to know. (Silence. Larry looks down) What's the matter?
LARRY:	Nothing. It's just that I anticipated that everything would go perfectly the first time.
HANK:	Larry, if everything went perfectly each time there

wouldn't be much challenge would there? As a troubleshooter, you've done your job. Now you can help Jerry understand the value of the new system and get them moving in the right direction. In the long run, Jerry will thank you for it. Larry we have more to cover, so let's meet back here after your meeting with Jerry.   (Looks at calendar)   How about 2:30?

LARRY: That's fine with me.

HANK: It sounds as if you've got things in hand in Personnel. It's not unusual to hit one or two snags occasionally. As long as you're on top of it and know what has to be done, that's what's important.   (Shakes Larry's hand)   I'll see you at 2:30.

LARRY: Thank you, sir.

Based on this discussion with Larry, how do you feel Hank rates as an effective listener?

_____

_____

_____

_____

What do you think might have happened had Hank rushed things along at the beginning of the conversation when Larry seemed hesitant in his communication?

_____

_____

_____

_____

Why did Hank's approach seem to pay off?

_____

_____

_____

Will Hank follow up with Larry as planned? Why?

_____

_____

_____

_____

CASE STUDY
ANALYSIS SUMMARY

The Systems and Methods Project
(Delegation—Subordinate Relationships)

Based on the discussion with Larry, how do you feel Hank rates as an effective listener?

Hank comes across as a superior listener. He is patient and reassuring. His probes indicate that he has concern for the task (he wants it to be done well) and has empathy for Larry (he wants him to succeed).

What do you think might have happened had Hank rushed things along at the beginning of the conversation when Larry seemed hesitant in his communication?

Larry would have been even more hesitant and might not have relaxed or demonstrated that he wished to get the job done on his own.

Why did Hank's approach seem to pay off?

Hank helped Larry build self-confidence. Hank demonstrated through his probes and his responses to Larry's comments that he believed Larry should and could do the job well.

Will Hank follow up on Larry as planned? Why?

Yes! Hank's desire for results makes it imperative and natural that he be concerned that the job is done right. However, he also has deep concern about Larry's ability to develop confidence in doing things on his own.

CASE STUDY ANALYSIS

The Purchasing Department Manager (Vendor Relationships)

You are the manager of a purchasing department who deals with a variety of vendors who provide services to your firm. You maintain the following standards in dealing with all vendors:

- You demand that representatives make an appointment to see you in advance.

- You obtain a Dun & Bradstreet report on any company with whom you are doing business for the first time.

- You require a financial statement for the past year of the firm's existence.

- You require a list of the principal accounts with whom the firm does business.

- You require a minimum of five business references.

- You will not purchase new materials or equipment without trying out the merchandise first. This means you place a small order initially until you determine that you are satisfied with the product and/or service.

- You seek quality products and service with a guarantee of nationwide delivery.

- You expect prices to be competitive.

- You normally will try out at least three services before making a final decision to go with a vendor.

Your primary concern is to obtain quality products/services at a competitive price and ensure timely deliveries to your nationwide offices. Recently the representative of a major supplier of business forms who has been trying for weeks to obtain your business made an appointment to meet with you in your office at 11:30 A.M. to introduce his product and service. You have been unhappy with the delivery service provided by the organization with whom you currently have a contract. The contract expires in three weeks.

The first five items on your requirements list have already been satisfied by the new vendor. The formalities of the initial greeting are concluded and you've embarked on a discussion of the vendor's services. Since your most critical need is timely deliveries, you wish to feel assured that this will not be a problem. In order to satisfy this need, you've given the representative a list of your national offices and specified that you require standard deliveries of forms on a weekly basis—each Saturday—unless otherwise notified. He assured you that would not be a problem. Then you mentioned that there might be special circumstances when immediate deliveries would be needed on a spot basis, i.e., occasionally when inventories run low unexpectedly and same-day service would be required. His reply was "Oh, don't worry about that. We're ready to take care of anything you need" in what you interpreted as an oversolicitous manner. He then asked who you were presently dealing with and why you felt you wanted to change services. You explained that the contract was about to expire and you were checking out other possibilities. At this point he stated his company had far superior services and asked what other firms you were checking with.

You were not satisfied with his response to your spot-delivery inquiry, found his criticism of the firm you currently deal with unduly harsh, and felt he was presumptuous in asking for the names of the other vendors with whom you are consulting.

What would you say next?

_____

_____

_____

_____

_____

_____

_____

_____

_____

_____

_____

_____

_____

CASE STUDY
ANALYSIS SUMMARY

The Purchasing Department Manager
(Vendor Relationships)

What would you say next?

I'd ask the representative why the names of other firms I'm checking with would be of interest to him. Unless his response to this fact-finding probe convinced me that this information was important to our discussion, I'd return to the question of spot deliveries.

Here I'd reemphasize that I require some kind of guarantee from him that same-day service in unusual circumstances is an absolute requirement of any forthcoming arrangement with his firm. If he's sincere about honoring my request he will likely indicate that he can include this information in a written contract. If he doesn't make this offer I'll request that the contract include a clause relating to same-day deliveries and see what he says.

No commitment has been made, and won't be until I'm satisfied that my requirements will be met.

Listening Implications

Managers learn from experience that not all representatives handle every situation to the manager's satisfaction. As illustrated in the above analysis, managers control and guide the listening process when they use relevant probes that help them obtain the information or commitments they need.

In this case study on-time delivery is the key factor in selecting a reliable vendor.

CASE STUDY ANALYSIS

The Supervisory Skills Instructor (Coaching)

You are the manager of a training department that has two instructors. One of the instructors teaches basic clerical skills (two years on job), the other teaches supervisory skills (has done this for three years). You've been with the department for two months, and have been evaluating the performance of your two instructors.

The supervisory instructor helped develop the course materials that are currently in use. You are pleased with the course content, but have encountered the following problems concerning the instruction:

* One full-day session has been given to date in leadership skills. Fifteen persons in supervisory jobs took the course (just completed last week). In almost every case the written evaluations submitted by the attendees have indicated a dissatisfaction with the instruction. Comments have included: "The instructor didn't seem genuinely interested in the subject"; "I didn't really get much out of it"; "Rather dull and boring." The instructor has not seen these as yet.

* You had decided not to audit the course initially, since you wanted to show that you had faith in the instructor's ability.

* Two managers phoned you today and asked, "Why do you give that course, my people didn't get much out of it?"

* In spot-checking with some of the managers, including

the two who phoned you, they indicated they never really had a problem with the instructor before. Most persons they had sent in the past had favorable things to say about the program.

You've decided to have an informal chat with the instructor.

What are your objectives in talking with the instructor?

_____

_____

_____

Have you any preconceived thoughts about what caused the negative reactions of the attendees? If "yes," what are they?

_____

_____

_____

What approach do you plan to use to satisfy your objectives?

_____

_____

_____

CASE PROBLEM
SUMMARY ANALYSIS

The Supervisory Skills Instructor
(Coaching)

What are your objectives in speaking with the instructor?

(1) Try to determine what caused the attendees to feel disenchanted with the course.

(2) Take whatever action the instructor and I agree on to ensure that the course is meeting the needs of the attendees and meeting standards for communicating with attendees.

Have you any preconceived thoughts about what caused the negative reactions of the attendees? If "yes," what are they?

I may have, but I'd better keep them out of my thinking process. Objectivity is a keynote to my relationships with the attendees and the instructor, and I must have a completely open mind in dealing with the person and the subject.

What approach do you plan to use to satisfy your objectives?

I'm new to the department, and this is the first time this course has been given since I took over my job. Also, the instructor has had a good track record with the course in the past. Nevertheless, I will come to the point immediately and reveal what the attendees and the managers have reported, then I'll want to get the instructors' opinion as to why the attendees reacted the way they did. I must also take care to ensure the instructor that my real concerns are to meet the objectives, i.e., (1) and (2) above.

It is conceivable that some managers might prefer to ask the instructor how he or she believes the session went before revealing the exact nature of the feedback. However, there are inherent dangers in following this kind of approach. Should the instructor respond by indicating that he or she believes everything went well, it is almost impossible not to end up putting the person on the defensive (and getting on a treadmill) when you finally reveal (which you must do) what the attendees thought. The listening process will be impaired just as soon as the element of contradiction is introduced, and meeting your intended objectives will be difficult to say the least. However, once you have acquainted the instructor with the facts at the outset, and then the instructor feels they are not justified, you can begin to work together through your probes to resolve the situation. Keep in mind that the attendees' feedback is a *mutual* concern. Telling it like it is up front, and seeking solutions together, is important to you both. This is true particularly since you're at a point in your working relationship where trust and commitment is being established.

CASE STUDY ANALYSIS

The Case of Bill Finnegan
(Performance Appraisal—Motivation)

A manager has completed a written appraisal of one of the supervisors on his staff, Bill Finnegan. Bill has worked with the manager for six months, and this is Bill's first formal appraisal.

The manager believes Bill has done a competent job. He sees Bill as a take-charge type who works long hours and comes in early to the office nearly every day. Bill has made some innovative contributions to the department operation and these have been duly noted by the manager.

A few of the less-experienced clerks in the department who report to Bill recently complained to you that they find him too aggressive. They indicated that Bill tries to take over their work and do it for them. They said it has been going on for a while, but had not said anything about it to anyone, including Bill, because they thought the problem might resolve itself. It still persists, however, according to them. The manager scheduled an appraisal interview with Bill to discuss his progress. The objectives for the interview included:

- Let Bill know he's doing a good job.

- Discuss the complaint made by the junior clerks, try to identify the problem, and seek agreement on a solution.

- Explore areas for Bill's future in the department and the company.

The interview is in progress. The manager has reviewed Bill's achievements and feels very comfortable with Bill's attitude toward the work and his progress.

When the subject of the junior clerks' complaints was addressed, Bill offered these explanations:

- He expressed disenchantment with their not having discussed the problem with him first.

- He indicated that he intercedes to help the clerks with their work occasionally in order to meet department schedules. When they fall behind he gives them a hand. He believes his actions are in the best interests of the department, since he's responsible for getting the work done well and on time.

- In response to further probes on the manager's part, Bill indicated that a few of the clerks are not as reliable as the senior persons who know what they're doing and don't give him any trouble. He also told the manager that he's trying to help the junior clerks be more self-sufficient by encouraging them to look up information in their training manuals when they have questions or make mistakes. "It's high time they got their act together and got serious about learning their jobs" was his comment.

At this point, the manager replied:

"Maybe you're expecting too much from them too soon, Bill. Why don't you think about spending some time with each clerk reviewing the areas where they're weak in their work, then, if they need it, give them some additional training so they'll do the tasks correctly. That should stop the complaints."

Bill looked straight at the manager for a few minutes without replying, then said:

"Okay! I'm not so sure it will work, but I'll try it if you want me to."

The manager added that he believed it was worth a try and proceeded to introduce the subject of Bill's future development.

Do you think Bill is convinced that the manager's solution is a good one? Why? Also, how seriously do you think he'll follow through on the manager's recommendation?

_____

_____

_____

_____

_____

_____

Would you have proceeded any differently if you were the manager? If "yes," what would you have done and why?

_____

_____

_____

_____

_____

_____

_____

_____

CASE STUDY ANALYSIS SUMMARY

The Case of Bill Finnegan (Performance Appraisal—Motivation)

Do you think Bill is convinced that the manager's solution is a good one? Why? Also, how seriously do you think he'll follow through on the manager's recommendation?

No . . . Bill is not convinced.

Bill's reply to the boss's suggestion indicates he doesn't really want to do the training and is merely bowing to the boss's request. The manager has not made any attempt to convince Bill of the logic behind his suggestion; therefore, it's likely that Bill may make only a pass at giving the junior clerks additional training. Since the manager didn't make an attempt to find out from Bill where the clerks were having problems, Bill doesn't have anything to get back to the manager about. Also, there is no planned follow-up implied by the manager, which may lead Bill to believe that the training is not a primary concern for either of them. As a result there's a good chance the problem will persist or just be swept under the table.

Would you have proceeded any differently if you were the manager? If "yes," what would you have done and why?

Instead of "telling" Bill what to do, I might have:

(1) Commented favorably on Bill's desire to help others get the work out on time.

(2) Acknowledge that senior persons may be more reliable, then indicate that perhaps they, like Bill himself, were new on the job once and may have had some tough times learning their jobs in the beginning. Emphasize that the newer clerks would benefit from guidance and encouragement.

(3) Through probes I'd ask Bill if there might be some other ways he could help bring the newer clerks up to snuff. By doing this Bill might volunteer that additional training might help. If Bill, instead, stuck to his guns about "looking things up in the manual," I'd ask for some specifics about the areas where the clerks seem to perform below standard. After Bill identifies the clerk's weak areas, I'd ask him if he believes new persons find such items tough to understand usually. I'd also want to know if new clerks might be skeptical about their ability to retain certain types of information about the work.

My motivation is to help Bill appreciate the need to coach patiently and fairly by giving his people personal attention from time to time. Bill needs to leave the meeting believing that the extra training may work. As the manager it is my obligation to get Bill talking about what is best for his people and guiding him toward approaches to the problem that we both feel are worth trying.

Listening implications

I'm interested in getting Bill to talk out solutions to the problem with the clerks. By listening to *his* ideas—and introducing my own at appropriate times in a nonthreatening, constructive way without imposing my will—Bill realizes that our interests in doing the job correctly are shared interests. The only difference between Bill's original approach and what we decide to try next is that we know the first way didn't work and we feel the new approach may have a better chance of working.

CASE STUDY ANALYSIS

The Lost Account (Telephone Communication/Customer Relations)

The manager of the sales department of a publishing house that specializes in research reports for industry is told by his assistant that a key account decided not to renew their subscription to the firm's technical writing service. Apparently the secretary to the president had broken the news just a few moments earlier when the assistant made a routine follow-up call to inquire about the renewal. The secretary told the assistant her firm was switching to a competitive service, then got off the phone before the assistant could ask for further details.

The manager and his staff had worked hard to land this account, a large international corporation. The one-year contract was to expire in three weeks and the renewal contract had been sent out as a matter of course last week.

The manager, who'd been on a prospecting jaunt nationally in an effort to generate new business and beef up sales, had just returned yesterday to his office. He's distressed about the decision not to renew on a number of counts. They are:

- The loss of this account means a sizable drop in income for the firm, which has already had a bleak quarter.

- There were no known complaints about the service, and the renewal had seemed like a foregone conclusion.

- The manager had sent a personal letter to the president only two weeks ago expressing his pleasure over having such a fine account and inviting the president to dine with the manager. No reply to the letter was received, nor had any follow-up been made by the manager.

- The manager is unhappy that his office learned of the decision not to renew in what appears to be such an informal, offhand manner.

The manager is determined to keep the account and makes an immediate phone call to the president. When the president gets on the phone, the conversation proceeds as follows:

Manager: Mr. Pritchard, this is George Johnson at Acme. I just learned from my assistant that your secretary phoned to tell us you're not renewing our service. I can't believe you'd want to change . . .

President: George, you've caught me at a very bad time, you'll have to pursue this some other time.

Manager: From what I can see we've met all your requirements in the past. Can't you tell me what happened? We really want your business.

President: You don't seem to understand; I can't speak with you now. Call me back tomorrow. (Hangs up)

What do you think of the manager's method of seeking to keep the account?

_____

_____

_____

_____

_____

_____

_____

_____

If you were the manager, what would you do? Why?

_____

_____

_____

_____

_____

_____

_____

_____

_____

CASE STUDY
ANALYSIS SUMMARY

The Lost Account—Customer Relations/Telephone Communications

What do you think of the manager's methods of seeking to keep the account?

It's weak and ineffectual. The phone call was made impulsively, with little, if any, forethought given to dealing with the situation.

If you were the manager, what would you do? Why?

Before taking any action, I'd want to be certain of a few things:

- Was my letter inviting the president to dinner sent?

- Was the renewal contract mailed?

- Were there no complaints about our service as reported?

My staff can help me get the answers to these questions. While I'm at it, I'd reread the dinner invitation letter to see what I'd written and recheck the contract to be sure it was in order. If there were any complaints whatsoever, I'd want to know what they were and what had been done about them.

I'd phone the president directly, and without mentioning the contract, try to set a date for our dinner engagement. If the president agreed to meet me for dinner, I'd approach him about the renewal in this compatible, social setting. If the president declines my dinner offer, I'd explain that I'd appreciate the chance to speak with him about the renewal contract and try to set up a meeting at his office.

Speaking about this matter in any form on the phone presents a risk I'm not prepared to take. The impersonality of the phone call on this important matter, which presents the possibility of an interruption at a critical point in the conversation, discourages me from talking about the subject on the phone. I could use some time (not much) to develop a strategy. In the meantime I'd find out which service the firm is planning to switch over to so I can do a thorough comparison of the two.

Listening implications

The manager showed serious listening deficiencies in the original call. No objectives were set, so it seems the manager rambles all over the place. Also, everything is "me, me, me." There's no concern shown for the president and the needs of his firm.

Certain matters don't lend themselves well to phone discussions. This is probably one of them. There's a better chance that each person can benefit from a face-to-face discussion. Even if the manager is unable to succeed in renewing the contract when they meet, he has a better chance of solidifying their relationship and trying again for the account at another time. Also, he may learn things about his operation that will help in his communications with other accounts.

CASE STUDY ANALYSIS

The Frustrated Chairperson— (Chairing a Meeting)

A manager is the chairperson of a committee comprised of five other department managers from his division. The division head has commissioned the group to solve some internal operating problems common to all five departments. In preparation for their first formal meeting the chairperson asked each member to plan to make a five-minute presentation on how the problems were being dealt with in their respective departments.

At the outset of the meeting the chairperson asked that each attendee withhold commentary until everyone had given his/her presentation. The meeting got off to a good start; however, as one manager began to speak, the secretary of the manager in whose conference room the meeting was held interrupted the proceedings. She announced that her boss had an urgent phone call, at which point that manager excused himself and left the room, returning just before the manager who was speaking concluded her remarks.

As the next speaker began his talk, the manager who had previously exited turned to the former speaker and raised a question about her operation. Had he not left the room, he would have known the subject had already been covered. In response to his question some managers looked agitated and one interjected, "We've already discussed that, so let's get on with it," whereupon the "absentee" manager looked daggers. At this juncture of the meeting, if you were the chairperson:

What would you do? Why?

_____

_____
_____
_____
_____
_____
_____

As chairperson, what can you do before the start-up of a meeting to discourage interruptions from outsiders?

_____

_____

_____

_____

_____

As chairperson, what should you do when a member of the group breaks an established rule of the meeting, e.g., asking a question when questions are to be tabled till the end of the meeting?

_____

_____

_____

_____

_____

_____

CASE STUDY
SUMMARY ANALYSIS

The Frustrated Chairperson
(Chairing a Meeting)

What would you do? Why?

Remind everyone that all questions were to be tabled to the conclusion of the session. Indicate to the inquiring manager that he may ask his question at that time, then turn the meeting back to the present speaker. Remind myself that I will not permit any additional interruptions.

In order to be fair to the group and, at the same time,

maintain my leadership position, I must stick to the rules. Since it is generally understood that attendees should not leave meetings without prior authorization, I would have been justified in imploring the manager to table the call and remain at the meeting.

As chairperson, what can you do before the start-up of a meeting to discourage interruptions from outsiders?

Let everyone attending know that for the expedience of time and to allow for concentration on the meeting subject everyone should plan to remain at the meeting until its conclusion. Ask the person whose facility is being used to remind his staff that once the door is closed there shall be no interruptions. Often, for lengthy meetings, a message board is set up for attendees to check at break times.

As chairperson, what should you do when a member of the group breaks an established rule of the meeting, e.g., asks a question when questions are to be tabled till the end of the meeting?

It's advisable to enforce the rule immediately, lest with one exception permitted, the rule becomes meaningless and unenforceable.

Listening implications

Once an acceptable rhythm or pattern of any meeting is broken it becomes much more difficult for attendees to concentrate on relevant issues/ideas. As the session leader the chairperson promotes *positive listening* by continually assessing the needs of the group as they relate to the meeting objective. The chairperson's behavior is the key to how effectively the group listens and participates.

CASE STUDY ANALYSIS

The Delegating Manager
(Delegation—Time Constraints)

A manager who feels burdened by what seems like an overwhelming number of tasks decides to keep a log of all tasks performed for a given week. After reviewing the log entries, he prepares a list of all the tasks that he believes can be handled by his secretary. The next morning the manager calls his secretary into his office and assigns some of the tasks to her. While describing what he wants done, the secretary seems a bit preoccupied.

As the week progresses the manager finds that the secretary is not doing the newly assigned tasks. Upon confronting her, she informs him that she wasn't too clear about what she should do and also isn't sure whether or not she can handle the items in addition to her regular work load.

What do you think went wrong?

_____

_____

_____

_____

What should the manager have done when he noticed the secretary was preoccupied?

_____

_____

_____

_____

*How should the manager deal with his secretary's not under-
standing what he wanted done and, at the same time, encourage her to incorporate the tasks into her work?*

_____

_____

_____

_____

_____

CASE STUDY
ANALYSIS SUMMARY

The Delegating Manager
(Delegation—Time Constraints)

What do you think went wrong?

The manager did not make an attempt to explain why
he was delegating the tasks nor did he show interest in
learning if and how the secretary might fit the tasks into
her work routine. The secretary may have gotten the impression that the manager "dumped" the work on her and, as a
result, showed indifference toward doing the tasks.

What should the manager have done when he
noticed the secretary was preoccupied?

The manager should have probed to find out why the
secretary seemed preoccupied. Had he been listening for
hidden messages, her preoccupation might have been viewed
as a possible signal that she was reluctant or hesitant to take
on additional work. The manager's probes might have
brought things out in the open and enabled the secretary to
address her misgivings about the tasks. The manager would
have had the chance to make it clear why the tasks needed

to be done and he could have explained how the secretary's assistance would be helpful. He also would have been able to deal with the problem of additional workload and, at the same time, convinced her that he cared about such things. Now they're both faced with round two.

How should the manager deal with his secretary's not understanding what he wanted done and, at the same time, encourage her to incorporate the tasks into her workload?

The manager should apologize for not having made the assignment clear and indicate that:

1) He is aware that since the new tasks have not been undertaken before they may seem strange.

2) He has confidence in her ability to take on new assignments and do them well.

He should also indicate that he'd like to explain the purpose of each task and describe how the tasks should be handled. He should then invite the secretary to ask questions and otherwise comment on each task as he proceeds. It is important that the manager be convinced that his secretary is willing to listen and accept his request to take on additional work; therefore, before proceeding, he ought to seek agreement about this approach.

CASE STUDY ANALYSIS

The Section Merger Proposal
(Peer Relationships)

Recently a memo was received by all section managers in which the department head asked for written proposals about how to improve operations. You are one of two section managers in your department.

You've taken a good look at your operation and believe you have some very positive suggestions to offer. One of your ideas is to merge the two sections into one.

Your research and experience have shown that a great deal of the work done by both departments is overlapping and believe you've come up with some substantial reasons for combining the two sections. You also feel that one manager can handle the work where two are presently needed, thus freeing a manager for another assignment.

You and the other section manager have maintained a good working relationship. You've had casual discussions about operational changes in the past, but have never put your heads together to work on a formal plan.

Today you are meeting with the section manager for lunch, at which time you plan to elicit his cooperation in working with you in submitting a joint proposal on the subject to the boss. As you sit down to lunch the manager opens the conversation by asking if you've gotten wind of the plans afoot for a company-wide layoff due to unsettled business conditions. He adds, "It's got me worried." You've heard nothing about a layoff, but know how rumors (founded and unfounded alike) such as this one can crop up.

What will you do or say that will encourage the other manager to work with you on the project?

_____

_____

_____

_____

_____

CASE STUDY ANALYSIS SUMMARY

The Section Merger Proposal
(Peer Relationships)

What will you do or say that will encourage the other manager to work with you on the project?

I can't ignore my counterpart's comment about the lay-off rumor. He appears genuinely concerned about losing his job, and this concerns me. He may view a merger of the sections—with one manager at the helm—as a threat to his security, and I don't want that to distort his thinking re the advantages to the department of combining our operations. My experience tells me that a rumor is a rumor until fact proves otherwise, so some kind of brief comment that puts such things in perspective is appropriate.

Once our conversation turns to work matters, I'd begin by using probes to find out how the other section manager is progressing with his proposal. It's possible that, without prompting, the other manager may indicate he believes the work of our sections overlaps in some ways. I'd also tell him about some of the things I'm thinking about and solicit his opinion. This kind of discussion should help both of us look at what we're doing in a constructive and positive light.

To introduce the merger proposition, I'd better start with open probes that will get the other manager to express his ideas about combining certain features of our sections' work. His responses to these probes will give me the needed clues to determine whether or not this is an opportune time to pursue the subject further.

Should I learn through our discussions that my counterpart has some convincing arguments in favor of keeping our operations separate and distinct, I'd reevaluate my thinking on the subject. After doing so, if I still believe the merger idea has merit, I'd reintroduce the subject—probably at a later time. Should the manager be so intensely anti-merger that he appears unwilling to come to any agreement about our working together on the project, I'd suggest he give it some further thought, then get back to him later.

However, if I'm convinced that the manager sees merit in merging the sections, I'd do the following:

- Review the advantages of combining the sections, including any ideas he may present.

- Stress that this is really an opportunity to contribute some original ideas for the department and get recognition from the boss.

- Dismiss any apprehensions either of us may have thought of regarding expendability by stressing that whichever one of us is chosen for the new managerial post it should be seen as a promotion (larger staff; increased responsibilities), and we should anticipate that our salary would be reviewed accordingly. Also, since this was our idea for improving operations, the other person logically would be considered for a responsible post somewhere else in the company.

What if the other manager is against the merger and I'm still convinced it should be done? Certainly I don't want to injure my relationship with my peer so it's important for both of us that I'm completely open about what I'm doing. I believe I have an obligation to give my boss the ideas that seem in the best interests of the department; therefore, I'd let the other manager know that I'll make the merger proposal in my report. When I disclose this I'd make it clear that I respect his opinion, reiterate why I think the merger will work, and indicate that it will be up to the boss to make the final decision.

Listening implications

All managers face delicate situations from time to time in their communications with others. When managers are honest and direct in expressing their belief in what they feel is just and proper, and show through their actions that they are fair-minded and considerate of others, both parties are more likely to want to listen to one another and develop strong interpersonal relationships. Listening doesn't occur when persons hold back and refuse to be supportive of one another. That's when the ears *and* the eyes close up and indifference takes hold.

CASE STUDY ANALYSIS

The Staff Meeting
(Managing the Boss)

Your boss has invited you to a staff meeting of managers from your division. One of the subjects on the agenda is the introduction of a new system which you designed that will be used in the departments managed by the attendees.

You are new to the company, and this is the first meeting you've attended with your boss, who has been quite supportive of your work. Your boss is chairing the meeting.

In preparation for the meeting the boss told you he would call on you to identify the features of the system and suggested you plan to tell the managers how the system would benefit their departments.

At the meeting the boss began his discussion of the new system by lauding you for your contributions. He also told the group why it was developed and that he believed it would be of great benefit to everyone. Then he indicated you were ready to tell them all about it.

When you completed your presentation the boss added, "Now it's time to tell you how to implement the system." At this point he began describing for each person what he believed they should do. His comments included some of your ideas, but also contained others you've not heard of before. Your initial reaction is one of surprise for you believe it is premature to discuss implementation plans at this meeting. The reaction of the group—they seem confused and agitated—substantiates your view.

As the boss continues you reflect back on your previous communications with him. You had developed a plan for implementing the system which you submitted in writing. Subsequently, when you asked for the boss's reaction, he told you to wait awhile until he thought it through. That was the last time he communicated with you on the subject of implementation.

You're uncomfortable, but believe it would be undiplomatic to try to stop the boss from proceeding further. On a few occasions he tries to obtain your help particularly when issues are raised about items you recognize as your ideas. Finally the boss senses things are getting out of hand and says, "We'd better get back together again and go over this again at another time. I'll set up another meeting."

As you leave the room the boss turns to you and says, "Well I guess we blew that one; why didn't you stop me sooner? Come by my office in an hour and let's talk about it."

What do you plan to say to the boss when you meet with him?

CASE STUDY
ANALYSIS SUMMARY

The Staff Meeting
(Managing the Boss)

What do you plan to say to the boss when you meet with him?

Before making any plans about what I might say to the boss, I must first determine my objectives for our upcoming discussion. I'd want to accomplish the following:

(1) Work with the boss in developing a systems implementation strategy that will work.

(2) Plan the next meeting of the manager group with *system implementation* as the theme. In this respect I'd be thinking of how to make the meeting successful. For instance, I'd consider proposing to the boss that each manager be asked to submit a written plan indicating how they'd implement the new system. They'd be instructed to have the plan submitted within a certain time. I'd volunteer to review the plans and draw conclusions about their feasibility. This would be communicated to the boss, after which we'd meet to get his ideas and organize an agenda for the managers' meeting.

When the boss and I meet, I'd let him introduce the subject of the recent managers meeting and see where he wants to take it first. The boss may be thinking along the same lines as I am, so I'd be prepared to offer my suggestions to back him up. I'm ready to be flexible and see what he wants to do. He may have a better plan. I can always introduce my ideas if I believe they are worthy of his consideration.

Without making an issue I'd propose that an agenda for the next meeting be given to the attendees so they'll be able to focus on our goals. Dwelling on what went wrong at the initial meeting is pointless—the agenda will give us the proper direction.

Listening implications

The boss's mismanagement of the first meeting may have shown him that he needs to be a better organizer and session leader if he's going to get good results. As a concerned manager who has an interest in making the new system work your best recourse is to convince the boss through your actions that you support him *and* the new system. The preferred way to do this is to show how objective you are by working with him to make the next meeting a success.

The attendees left the first meeting somewhat disenchanted and confused, and may have developed the notion that things are not likely to improve at a second meeting. The best way to counteract any attitudinal problems on their part is to plan a new meeting where the same pitfalls will not be encountered. The chances are that the attendees will respond with interest, listen, and participate when they see by the boss's actions that things have been righted.

CASE STUDY ANALYSIS

The National Operations Manager (Delegation—for Developmental Reasons)

A national operations manager for an automotive parts manufacturing firm is impressed with the progress made by one of the junior clerical employees in the department. As part of the clerk's on-job development the manager has chosen to ask the clerk to conduct a telephone survey of operations managers in their plants to determine how the new system is working. The decision to conduct the survey is predicated on the feedback from three plant managers who reported kinks in the system.

The manager has called the clerk into the office to discuss the survey. An account of the discussion follows:

Manager: Good morning, Pete, thanks for coming by.

Clerk: Good day, sir.

Manager: I could use your help in determining how effectively our new automotive parts system is working in our plants. I'd like to explain what I think you could do.

Clerk: Yes! I'd be glad to help.

Manager: Good! This should be valuable experience for you, and also be helpful to the department.

Let me go back to the beginning. . . . The new procedure has been in effect four weeks now (while the manager is talking, the clerk begins taking notes on a pad he'd brought along). Initially, the foremen in our plants believed it would work beautifully, but now three of the offices have indicated there are a few kinks.

I'll be making a tour of all our plants next week and it's important that I know before I leave what problems they've encountered with the procedure.

Here's what I'd like you to do. . . . Telephone the operations manager in each one of our plants and find out how the procedure is working.

Clerk: I see. . . . What questions do you want me to ask?

Manager:	I'm not sure yet. That's where you should begin. I'd like you to read the procedure in its entirety and develop a set of questions you could ask the managers.
Clerk:	I'm not really familiar with the new procedure. Will that create a problem?
Manager:	I don't think so, Pete. You have the technical background in automotive parts operations. That should be sufficient.
Clerk:	What shall I do about my regular work?
Manager:	I'm not sure how long it will take to complete this assignment. I believe you'll have to get into it first before we can determine how it will affect your work. The time you'll need will include reading the procedure and becoming familiar with it, noting the questions you think you should ask and making calls. Right now I'm more concerned with the questions you should ask.
Clerk:	What problems did the three branches report so far?
Manager:	That's a good question. My secretary has that information . . . you can check with her. Interestingly, all three plants reported different problems.
Clerk:	What is your deadline for my getting back to you with my estimate on the time needed and the questions I think should be asked?
Manager:	This is Monday. . . . I'd like that by Thursday morning. Can you do that?
Clerk:	Yes . . . I believe I can. (Pause) If I want to check out anything first with the three branches, may I do that?
Manager:	Certainly you may.

Clerk: Fine! I'll get on it right away.

Manager: If you need me for anything, let me know. Thank you, Pete.

Clerk: You're quite welcome.

Based on this discussion, how confident do you believe the manager is in Pete's being able to handle this assignment? Why?

_____

_____

_____

_____

_____

_____

_____

Do you think the manager is a positive listener? *Why? Do you think the clerk is a* positive listener? *Why?*

Manager: _____

_____

_____

_____

Clerk: _____

_____

_____

_____

_____

CASE STUDY
ANALYSIS SUMMARY

The National Operations Manager
(Delegation—for Developmental Reasons)

Based on the discussion, how confident do you believe the manager is in Pete's being able to handle this assignment? Why?

Highly confident! The types of questions asked by Pete show he's interested in doing the job and in doing it well.

Do you think the manager is a *positive listener*? Why?

Yes! The manager projects high expectations about the clerk's performance, is supportive, gives the full, objective story about his need for feedback from the offices, and answers each of the questions raised by the clerk in a straightforward manner.

Do you think the clerk is a *positive listener*? Why?

Yes! Pete's probes tell the manager that Pete has a commitment to get all the information needed to handle the project effectively. He also came prepared to take notes.

Listening implications

Managers often feel blessed when members of their staff are self-motivated and need very little direction in doing their work. However, these same managers should not lose sight of the way they themselves contribute to sustaining the progressive attitudes of their employees. The managers create the environment in which persons can use and develop their talents. In such cases the willingness to listen becomes automatic because there's nothing to lose and most always something to be gained.

INDEX

ABOUT THE AUTHOR

Warren Reed has been a training manager for twenty-five years at such firms as E.F. Hutton and Paine Webber. He has taught at the New York Institute for Finance and at New York University, from which he received the Outstanding Service Award. He was also the recipient of the Torch Award from the American Society for Training and Development. Since 1982 he has headed his own consulting firm in New York.